Today's Woman, Tomorrow's Church

Today's Woman Tomorrow's Church

by
Kaye Ashe

THE THOMAS MORE PRESS
Chicago, Illinois

In memory of Julia,
who taught me to believe and to hope

Contents

(continued)

FOREWORD

IN 1972 Sr. Albertus Magnus McGrath wrote for the Thomas More Press a book entitled *What a Modern Catholic Believes about Women.* Years before in a history classroom she had begun to shape my image of woman and of Catholic women. We continued our conversations when I returned to Rosary College as her colleague. She would be happy, I believe, to know that this book will join hers on the shelves of those who share our conviction, my enduring one and hers till the moment of her death, that the question of women in church and society is one of the most crucial of these times.

Although the focus of this volume is on women in the Catholic church, women of other religious traditions will, no doubt, find in its pages echoes of their own experience. Still, I should clarify the fact that most often when I use the term "church" I am referring to the Catholic Church. This is simply in the interests of brevity. I am acutely conscious of the fact that "church" embraces a much wider reality than is represented by the Catholic Church. Women in the church in that larger sense have much to gain through dialogue and through united action. I hope this book will in some ways provide a basis for both.

Unless other sources are quoted, the women who speak in these pages are those who answered a seven-page questionnaire dealing with their experience as women in today's Catholic church.

9

Eighty-two women responded, often with deep feeling and after long reflection. They represent different age groups, economic backgrounds and geographical locations. Where they gave permission I have quoted them by name. Otherwise I have respected their desire to remain anonymous.

I must thank each of the eighty-two women who took time to share their belief, hope, and pain, as well as the women who agreed to lengthy interviews in which they generously revealed themselves and their evolution in the church. I thank also the members of the St. Giles Family Mass Community for describing their "parish within a parish;" several friends and members of my community who offered helpful editorial comments, especially Sr. Benvenuta Bras; Patricia Klbecka for typing the manuscript; and numerous women for countless conversations in which we sparked one another and imagined a church and a world in which all people were responsibly and gloriously free.

INTRODUCTION

Which Women? Which Church?

TO reflect on Catholic women in today's church is to confront a wonderfully complex reality. Perhaps it was never a simple task, but until the mid-sixties it seemed simple. A girl baptized in 1930 learned her catechism in grade school, was warned of the dangers of sex in high school even as she timidly experimented with mild or heavy petting, looked forward to a permanent marriage as soon as possible after graduation from high school or college and to welcoming as many children as "God would send," or else considered a life of service in a religious community where she would teach or nurse. There were few crises of faith, and apparently little resistance to the destiny of finding identity and fulfillment in the role of loyal wife and mother or of obedient Bride of Christ. This girl, young woman, and mature adult did not differ notably in her upbringing and in her aspirations from the long generations of Catholic women who preceded her. All were, ideally, either submissive wives who were nevertheless queens in their domestic spheres or docile religious who were to know the joys of spiritual motherhood. In this spirit, Pope John Paul I, while Patriarch of Venice (1969-1978, that is after Vatican Council II),cautioned mothers to carry out their humble but wonderful

duties without complaint lest their daughters rebel
against housework. He gave voice to the desire of a
husband who:

> ...will always want his spouse to have a beautiful
> appearance and a beautiful figure, to move gracious-
> ly and to dress elegantly; he will also be proud if she
> has read Shakespeare and Tolstoy, but he is also
> practical and likes to eat well so he will be doubly
> happy if he discovers that in addition to a beautiful
> spouse he has acquired a priceless queen of the
> kitchen and queen of sparkling floors and of a house
> made beautiful by delicate hands and of children
> brought up as living flowers.[1]

The Western middle or upper class woman to whom
this advice was addressed is likely to greet it today
with laughter or a despairing groan, while it fails
utterly to take into account the experience of
thousands of working women whether in the West or
in the Third World.

The unreality of John Paul I's words less than a
decade after he wrote them is a measure of the
transformation in consciousness among Catholic
women in the last twenty years. They question or reject the assumptions behind the Pope's admonition,
assumptions which many shared in the 50's: women
must be beautiful to be acceptable; if educated, their
intellectual accomplishments are largely ornamental
and their object is to reflect well on their husbands;
women's work consists in cooking and cleaning;
they have a monopoly on this work and should per-

form it joyfully lest their children be tempted to reject the joys of childbearing and domesticity.

Some of the same forces that have wrought this change in women have also effected a re-thinking of the nature and mission of the church, the role of authority within it, the role of priesthood, ministry, liturgy, and canon law.

The church that emerged from Vatican Council II was in general one much more aware of and sensitive to changing social structures, one which emphasized collegiality over rigid authority, and saw itself as a community whose members ministered to one another and to all in faith, hope, and love, a community in constant need of reconciliation and renewal.

The process which has resulted in a new vision both of women and of church has not been painless, and it isn't over. Contradictions between the new self-understanding and stubborn old structures and practices plague many Catholic women in their parishes, in their workplace, and in their homes. Some of their frustration as church members is shared, of course, by all in the church who are impatient with the slow progress in translating the theological perception of Vatican Council II into meaningful practice in the parishes and dioceses of the United States. Women in the church have not shared equally, however, in the women's revolution or in church renewal. To write, then, of American women in the post-conciliar church raises a host of questions. Who is this woman? What is this church?

The Modern Catholic Woman

The modern American Catholic woman no longer presents an easily sketched profile. She probably has fewer children than her mother, if she is married. She may be back in college working for a degree she abandoned in the 60's. She is more likely than not working outside the home. She may be divorced, and remarried. She may be single and determined to remain so. She may be active in a parish that welcomes her collaboration in ministry, or stunned to learn that her services as lector, for instance, are no longer required. She may be a missionary who ministers with the poor in ways that make the church visible and credible, or a pastoral associate working out the problems of being the only woman on a parish team. She may find that male-dominated liturgies and church language that exclude her are no longer tolerable, and so seek women's prayer and study groups. If she lives in a suburb, her experience of church is different than if she lives in a ghetto of the inner city. If she is a self-acknowledged lesbian, her relationship to the church may be tenuous. Whoever she is, she is less likely today than in the 50's or early 60's, to look to direction from the hierarchy or local clergy in order to determine her moral and ethical stances. Rather than attempt a composite profile of American Catholic women, which would be meaningless were it possible, it will be worthwhile to look briefly into the lives and present hopes and frustrations of individual women in today's church. Their experiences will illustrate the range of women's activities and the evolution which has marked their lives during a tumultuous period of church history. First, however, let us look at the church which has played a part in shaping the lives of those women, and which they help form as part of the community of believers.

The Post-Conciliar Church

Just as it is easier to describe the American Catholic woman of pre-Vatican Council II days, so the church of those days presented a seemingly unified and united facade. This church was dominated by scholastic theology, was suspicious of other religions and even of other Christian churches, saw itself as removed from the world, and indeed condemned modern civilization and particularly anything that smacked of liberal, progressive thought. Ministry was considered to be the affair of the clergy. The laity attracted to "Catholic Action" were under the careful supervision of the clergy and were considered to be participating in the proper work of the hierarchy. Centralization of the church was extreme, and the hierarchical arrangement of its members rigid. Church practices and teaching gave the appearance of invulnerable solidity, and the average Catholic thought of these practices and teachings as dating from forever and destined to remain reassuringly static because invincibly true. The Mass was in Latin; it wasn't a bad idea to say the

rosary while attending it. The Bible wasn't as sure a
guide as Tradition. Sisters wore habits and lived in
convents. Catholics didn't divorce, or if they did they
didn't remarry; they didn't practice birth control, or
if they did it was the sanctioned rhythm method or
the fool-proof abstinence method. They fasted in
Lent and abstained every Friday. Catholic mothers
didn't ordinarily work; father was the head, mother
the heart of the home. Catholic children went to
Catholic schools. Mixed marriages were frowned
upon and could not take place in the sanctuary. Outside the church there was no salvation.

We are familiar with what followed Pope John
XXIII's call for an Ecumenical Council and for an examination and renewal of Catholic life, and of the
church's structures, theology, ministry, liturgy, and
relation to other churches and to the world. The
dialogue that took place throughout the church on
the eve of the Second Vatican Council revealed both
the deep questioning and dissatisfaction that lay just
below the surface of Catholic life, and the desire of
many for official recognition and encouragement of
the work of formerly suspect theologians, biblical
scholars and liturgists.

The conciliar documents led Catholics into a new
age, one in which their church, rather than con-
demning the modern world, read in it "signs" of
God's unfolding revelation. Ministry was to be
everyone's concern. Parish councils, priests' senates
and national bishops' councils made inroads on cen-
tralized power and decision-making. Church and

doctrine, it became clear, were historical realities that have developed, changed, evolved and would continue to do so. The Council affirmed modern methods of interpretation of the Bible and placed scripture, tradition and the church's magisterium in much more nuanced relationship to one another. And, closer to the everyday lives of Catholics, parishes revitalized their liturgies, calling on the meaningful participation of their members.

The atmosphere of change, renewal and hope; the honest recognition of today's problems; the acceptance of the insights of modern scholarship not only in theology, scripture, and liturgy but also in psychology and sociology had a profound impact on every facet of the church. The laity began to play more active roles in ministry, to challenge paternalism even further, and to seek entrance into decision-making at all levels. Religious, at the invitation of the Council, examined their constitutions, stripping them of practices and restrictions which were out of tune with contemporary self-understanding and today's ministerial needs, and called one another to greater fidelity to the gospel. The new insistence on personal autonomy, openness, freedom, and flexibility on the part of laity, priests and religious alike dismayed some, who saw in the Council and the response to it less a renewal than a frightening collapse of order and authority.

But for the most part, the Council and its effects on the church of the 70's energized and encouraged its membership and led many to believe that items remaining on the agenda would be satisfactorily resolved before long: the question of birth control, of divorce and remarriage, of mixed marriages, of married clergy, and of minorities' and women's full acceptance into ministry and church governance. We know that these questions have not been solved in the intervening years, and that impatience with the ambivalence of the Council proceedings and with the pace of renewal led many out of the priesthood and religious life and some out of the church. If the twenty years since the opening of the Second Vatican Council have taught us anything, they have taught us that renewal is a continuous process and that far from being accomplished at the Council's end, it has barely begun.

In 1962 the Council launched a monumental effort to bring the church into the modern era and to adapt its methods and its message to the needs of today's world, while simultaneously returning to the fresh spring of the gospel. We have in the intervening years enjoyed the fruits of this effort in the forms of new growth in personal responsibility, dialogue with other Christians, more meaningful liturgies, and revitalized and mutually enriching ministries. We have also seen that renewal does not proceed universally at a gratifyingly steady pace and that some of the hope and promise born in the 60's has been dampened if not extinguished.

Hans Küng and Richard McBrien, among others, have articulated what many Catholics have experienced in the years since the Council: a divorce between those who still conceive of the church as a hierarchically arranged institution with the Pope, bishops and clergy at the top bearing the responsibility to teach and discipline their flocks, and those who see it as a community of equals united in a mutual relationship of service; between those who fear for the identity and unity of Catholics in the changes which have accompanied the modernization of the church and those who push for further change, and more openness and freedom. The position of these two groups differs in predictable ways on the issues of birth control, divorce and remarriage of Catholics, a married clergy and the ordination of women. Apart from these issues, there are different expectations at the opposite ends of the two poles as to the church's role in politics, its prophetic task, its duty to name oppression and to work for its over-throw.

In this divided church, women are concentrated in large numbers at the end of the spectrum which seeks greater declericalization, flexibility, realism, and credibility. Women in the church, in general, are less concerned with the subtleties of canon law than with the dynamics of social interaction; they are less preoccupied with dogmatic definitions than with human need. They are learning, too, to express their own needs with greater insistence and less guilt.

At this point, it will be useful to enter into the lives of a few contemporary Catholic women. The lives of seven women will not exhaust the truth about women's experience in today's church, but seeing some real women in action, hearing them reflect on the part church plays in their view of the world, and sharing their hopes and fears will have the advantage of giving flesh and blood to what might otherwise remain too general and too abstract.

Chapter One

PROFILES

THE women whose words and lives inspire this chapter will not speak for every woman or every category of woman in the American church. Absent, for instance, is the woman whose contact with the church is minimal, perhaps because the church's ritual and pronouncements have become meaningless for her. Absent, too, is the wife and mother who generously volunteers her services in parish activities, but who may not have had the time or opportunity to examine in much depth either her own faith life or theological and pastoral developments since Vatican II. These women will find their voices in later chapters. Meanwhile, the women who appear in this chapter will give some idea of the problems and frustrations as well as of the gifts, vitality, and the depth of American Catholic women.

TERESITA WEIND: PASTORAL MINISTER

Teresita Weind is a tall, lean black woman whose quiet serenity is transformed into vibrant energy when she steps into a pulpit and shares with the congregation the powerful, the healing Word of the Lord. The congregation she faces, 20 percent black and 80 percent white, gathers in St. Catherine of

Siena-St. Lucy in Oak Park, Illinois. Teresita serves
as pastoral minister and is responsible for adult
Christian inititation. In her seven years as director of
the Catechumenate program she has introduced
about sixty people (75 percent black; 25 percent
white) into active parish life.

Teresita's faith as a child was nourished in the
Baptist church. Her grandmother, a fervent Baptist,
served as a role model in her religious practice. She
attended a Catholic elementary school, however, and
despite her mother's disapproval, persisted
throughout grade school in wanting to be received
into the Catholic church. The young Baptist became
Catholic in seventh grade, soon enough to qualify for
and to actually become May Queen in eighth
grade—a heady moment for a recent convert!

Teresita entered the Sisters of Mary of the Presen-
tation at the age of eighteen and served as a
registered nurse. The mid-and-late 60's were years of
transition which led her out of nursing and into
another congregation, the Sisters of Notre Dame de
Namur of Cincinnati. Since then she has worked
with the poor of Cabrini Green in Chicago, "surfacing hope, engendering faith," and has served as the
diocesan liturgical coordinator for black parishes in
Chicago. Her present pastoral ministry in a progressive and alive suburban parish gives scope to the
exercise of her considerable gifts and to the realization of some of her goals as she creates church with
the parish team and parish members.

What are these gifts? First of all, a love for scripture, a grasp of the heart of its message, and an ability to communicate it in a voice and with a style that quickens the listener and demands a response. Teresita's early exposure to dynamic Baptist preachers was not lost on her. Her sensitivity to a racially mixed congregation makes her conscious of the need to temper the style, but the cadences, lyricism, metaphors, and soul of the Baptist tradition are unmistakable. She often concludes with a Gospel song in a voice which is another facet of her gifts. Second is her ability to grasp and to communicate the many levels of meaning in Sacramental ritual. Teresita's own faith finds easy expression in liturgy and symbol, and it is in well-celebrated eucharists that she finds her most rewarding prayer experiences. "Bread broken and shared and the cup passed among believers," she says, "becomes for me not only a sign of union in community but of oneness with the broken and the pained of the entire world."

And what are her goals as minister? To contribute to the church's renewal through the initiation of adults into Catholicism and the formation of leaders among the laity. She would like to see the spread of racially-mixed base communities where people can come to know and trust one another and grow in awareness of social justice issues, "all in the context of sharing faith as disciples of the Lord Jesus." Here in these base communities she finds a source of personal renewal and an ideal setting for the development of lay leadership.

Teresita's self-identity is closely related to her iden-

tity as member of a church community and as
minister. This closeness, however, does not preclude
an ability to look critically at the church and to regret
its slowness and its lack of staying power in effecting
social change whether in the areas of the equality of
the races and sexes, the immorality of violence and
of the nuclear arms race, or the dignity of life and
sexual responsibility. She feels confident to act on
her own conscience should there be a discrepancy
between it and certain papal and episcopal pronouncements, especially where these reveal insen-
sitivity or blindness to the realities of the local
church or the missionary church. The polarity between the Roman curia and the local churches is
most apparent, she feels, on the questions of a married clergy, real respect for women, and the status of
the divorced and remarried.

Teresita Weind is representative of scores of
women whose presence on pastoral teams has
brought new life and hope to parishes. She has been
luckier than many in being fully integrated in the
team, although as a woman her preaching gifts are
exercised without the approval of the diocese and
her position in the pulpit is, therefore, never assured.
She sometimes thinks ordination might be desirable
since it would allow a fuller exercise of ministry but,
like most women ministers, resists any temptation to
step into the old clerical model.

The vitality of the church's future ministry will be
linked to the affirmation of the many women who,
like Teresita, bring to it the kind of compassion and

sensitivity which enable them to say with Mari
Evans (a black poet), "Look on me and be renewed."

DOROTHY McINTYRE: SOCIAL ACTIVIST

Vatican II was barely over and Dorothy McIntyre
was on her mark and ready to go. Her parish and its
pastor, however, didn't share her enthusiasm for
exploring the Council's documents in depth and
translating them into action. She helped form a
group of twenty-five families from various parishes
in Chicago's western suburbs whose goal it was to
form a worshipping community ready to share "the
joys and the hopes, the griefs and the anxieties"
(opening words of the Pastoral Constitution on the
Church in the Modern World) of humankind, and
especially of the poor and the oppressed. Fr. Tom
Payton, a Maryknoll priest, celebrated a weekly
eucharist with the group which baptized itself the
Religious Education Community. He provided
leadership for the group from 1965 till 1981, and
since then group members themselves have prepared
the Sunday liturgies.

Dorothy McIntyre's faith and zeal for social
change were given impetus by the reflection of the
church of the 60's, but the official church has been
too slow for her in the formation of lay leaders and in
steady commitment to the kind of social change it
preaches. REC and the Peace and Justice Center in
Wheaton which it helps support is church for her
now, a church free of clericalism and of

authoritarian control. The Center brings together
people concerned about a wide range of issues: El
Salvador, Chilean refugees, disarmament, the draft,
prisons, women's liberation, hunger. They study the
issues and act through the Center and through a People's Resource Center. Volunteers give free crisis
counselling, organize workshops, vigils, ecumenical
gatherings, and have attempted to meet some of the
needs of the victims of recent governmental
priorities by opening food pantries in DuPage
County and running seminars on topics such as
money management techniques and good nutritional
habits.

The search of the 60's separated Dorothy McIntyre
from parish structures and from the official church
for a number of reasons. One of them was the growing realization that the clergy tended to be either
patronizing or terrified of bright women with a
strong sense of self. The gospel message of liberation, of growth in wholeness was often belied in
parish practice where women were concerned. The
call to servanthood was loud; the call to strength,
leadership, initiative, and creativity all but inaudible.
And yet, in Dorothy's eyes, women are the change
makers and in women rests whatever hope there is to
replace the violence and destruction of our present
technological, political and economic systems with
concern for human need.

"But no one needs permission to minister,"
observes Dorothy, "and women need not await a
conversion of the clergy in order to act now out of

their own experience." Dorothy, profoundly affected by the women's movement, removed herself from jarring encounters with representatives of clergy and hierarchy to form a church with couples who shared hers and her husband's concerns. If the conditioning of a patriarchal society persists in REC, at least there is an honest struggle to recognize and overcome it.

If Teresita Weind represents those women who are working fruitfully within parish structure, Dorothy McIntyre represents those for whom church and catholic (with small c's) are still meaningful terms but who felt compelled to move outside the traditional structures in order to find the freedom to respond authentically to the Gospel.

ROSEMARIE BORRELLI: CHARISMATIC

One of the sources of renewal for Catholics since Vatican II has been the charismatic movement. Women in large numbers have found the spirit of freedom and spontaneity in worship and the strong community ties of the movement a source of spiritual joy and growth. RoseMarie Borrelli is one of them. A convert to Catholicism in her high school days, RoseMarie later became disillusioned with inadequate homilies and with the emphasis on rules, regulations and structure. Her faith was re-kindled in 1964 at a Billy Graham revival meeting. She spent the years 1964-1971 in quiet study of the Bible and then discovered a charismatic prayer group, "The Children of Light," in which she has played an active

role ever since. She felt called to minister, especially
to women, through the healing of memories, and
sees herself above all as a pray-er, "a daughter who
fulfills the Father's vision."

RoseMarie's sources of spiritual growth are the
time-honored ones of the eucharist, both in her
parish and with her prayer group, consistent prayer,
alone and with others, and spiritual direction. She
has relied on healing of memories to free her from
the bitterness she carried into adulthood from an
unhappy childhood, and turns frequently to scripture to deepen God's grace and knowledge within
her. "I spend an hour each morning before going to
work," she explains, "reading scripture and being
quiet before the Lord." Her hopes for herself as an
active church member are to continue to teach and
give workshops, to communicate what she under-
stands to be the biblical view of men's and women's
role in the family and in the church, to help more
people move toward freedom and spiritual renewal,
and to become herself more obedient to the Lord as
an intercessor.

The charismatic movement provides a favorable
milieu for the laity to assume co-responsibility in
ministry with the ordained. RoseMarie's gifts of
inspiration, prayer, prophecy, wisdom and teaching
have found full scope in her prayer group, inner
healing sessions, and individual counseling.
RoseMarie would like to see the spiritual reawak-
ening which occurs in charismatic circles brought
into Sunday liturgies. This would be possible if

seminarians were offered a different sort of training. As ordained priests they would preach more freely and would allow time for spontaneous, inspirational prayer rising from the congregation. The laity, male and female, would be called upon to give homilies and to prophesy. In the church that RoseMarie envisions, priests would have the option to marry, and married couples would determine freely and without guilt the type of birth control to practice.

RoseMarie's view of male/female relationships stems more from her fundamentalist background than from recent Catholic thought. She sees the relationship as essentially hierarchical. Males rule; females obey. Strong women are likely to be described as controlling and manipulative. RoseMarie sees the women's movement as dangerous and undermining of the divine order in which males lead and have the primary roles in family, church and state. She speaks of "Jezebel" and "Ahab" spirits abroad; that is, forceful women who usurp men's positions and weak men who allow it to happen. For her, the healing of women often means reconciling them to a place of subordination, reminding them of the need to be meek, gentle, obedient and long-suffering. The hierarchical arrangement of the sexes does not deprive women in the church of their right to speak, minister, teach, and participate in decision-making, but their position and authority are subject ultimately to men's, as are a wife's to her husband's. Male rule will be tempered and will be happily borne by women whether in the home or the church if men are "in right relationship to the Lord."

The social issue which RoseMarie sees as most urgent is related to her understanding of gender roles. She believes the church should speak out against the women's movement, and should emphasize the role of the husband and father as spiritual leader of the family. This, she feels, would go a long way toward restoring the church to unity. She is careful to point out that her views on the correct relationship of the sexes may not be those of the charismatic movement at large, but she believes they have a solid scriptural base.

Whether or not they agree with the divine right of males to rule, a variety of women in today's church, like RoseMarie, find strength and peace in charismatic community, and in pentecostal prayer, study groups, and retreats.

KATIE STANLEY: MINISTRY TO "FORGOTTEN PEOPLE"

Katie Stanley's relgious roots lie in the Southern Baptist church, but she turned from church and Christianity in her teens, when, confused, hurt, and bitter, she had to flee with her family from their large farm in Union Springs, Alabama. The Ku Klux Klan threatened their lives and forced them out; Katie's father had been active in the civil rights movement of the late 40's. Katie emerged from this experience with a deeply shaken faith and an intense hatred of whites.

Only the memory of a Catholic sister she had heard speak in Montgomery, Alabama, at an inter-racial conference in 1949 helped keep a small spark of hope and faith alive. This was the first white person she had heard express concern about injustice and about the poor. When she moved to Chicago in 1951 it was, perhaps, this memory which led her to accept a young priest's suggestion to work at St. Scholastica's, a school directed by Benedictine Sisters. Here, in an atmosphere of respect, care and concern among equals, her faith in Christ and humanity was restored. She moved on from St. Scholastica's to a position with Headstart in the Archdiocese of Chicago in 1968.

Katie attended Catholic services for years before becoming a "card-carrying" Catholic. After a long period of testing, she was convinced that in the Catholic church she would find the ministry she wanted and the community she sought. Father Robert Backis initiated her into the St. Charles L'Wanga parish community in 1975.

Katie, who knew from the inside what it meant to be a victim of an oppressive social and economic system, wanted her work and life to touch others who have been hurt, broken, and on the edge of numb despair. In 1977 she began to work with Fr. Backis as co-director of the Lifeline Center, the social justice and evangelization arm of the parish. They knew it was important that the center be visible in the community and accessible to all, so they opened it first in a storefront and moved later to a building

which they share with the public library in the midst
of the Robert Taylor Homes. Here Katie Stanley has
helped organize CETA programs to educate, train
and provide employment for young blacks, a Super
Start program for teenage mothers, tutoring and
counseling programs, and arts festivals in which
talented black students have performed or exhibited
work which grew out of courses in music, African
dance, drama and photography. Katie Stanley's basic
goal is, however, to nourish in the forgotten people
of Robert Taylor Homes a deep sense of their self-
worth built on the conviction that "Christ is alive
and well."

Lifeline Center's director believes that only the
church can make inroads on the hunger, crime, rape,
wife and child abuse, drug and alcohol addiction,
and the poverty which underlies all of this in the
over-crowded, rundown, bleak public housing on
Chicago's South Side. Politicians are neither free nor
committed to changing it, she says, and she scoffs at
Reagan's "safety net." When Christian churches
band together and concentrate their energy and their
influence on the issue of poverty, then government
may respond. For Katie Stanley this is the central
ethical and moral issue, and it is more immediate
than questions of birth control, abortion, or the
limitation of nuclear arms. More immediate because
it helps explain abortion, child abuse, battered wives,
crime and drugs, and more basic because it has to do
with the elemental need of food and shelter. "Let's
talk about *these* issues," she urges. "In Lent, let's talk

about the poor who are crucified every day." Where does this woman renew her own spiritual strength? In prayer, of course, in "talking to the Lord," and in the kind of community witness that takes place in the "Christ Renews His Parish" weekends. Praying together, sharing both their pain and strength, Catholics black and white, rich and poor, lay and religious from several different parishes come to realize more perfectly during these weekends the "freedom of the children of God." For Katie Stanley this means basically freedom from distrust, freedom from a clique mentality, freedom from prejudice.

Katie Stanley's is the voice of a woman in the church who consciously ministers as a member of a faith community in which she sees the role of the laity slowly becoming more important. But to the question, "Have you found full scope in the church for your ministerial gifts?" she was quick to answer, "No." Being a lay woman (married and with children), a black, and a convert have all militated against her full acceptance as a responsible, competent minister and decision-maker in the church. Blacks still look too often to whites for validation and approval; women still look too often to men for the same things. Katie Stanley is looking for the same acceptance in the church that is offered a white religious or priest. She resents the fact that her decisions are often not respected by the predominantly male parish council, and finds it hard to understand why women, without whom there would be no church, have to struggle so hard against a discrim-

ination that is no less painful in its effects for being
unconscious in its practitioners. She has shared in
the struggle of women to be women and remain in
the church, smarting under unexamined assumptions that women do things haphazardly, or that they
should do the more menial, invisible tasks whether
in running the parish bingo or preparing the liturgy.
She looks forward to the day when women will be ordained because she believes that women, especially,
are agents of change. Ordained or not, Katie Stanley
is herself an agent of change, a woman whose quiet
work, intelligence, and heart, make a difference to
the young and old who suffer, struggle and dream in
the nightmare housing wrought by government
"planning."

MARY YU: YOUNG, SINGLE, COMMITTED, AND QUESTIONING

Mary Yu was just seven years old when the Second
Vatican Council came to a close in 1965. Unaware of
the church's monumental effort to update and of the
atmosphere of change, she experienced parish and
parish school mainly as the hub of community activity. She belonged to a small Chicago parish whose
125 families knew one another well. Being Catholic
for Mary was then largely a social affair, a cultural
given, part of the Mexican heritage that is hers
through her mother.

At the Catholic high school she attended, Mary
describes the religious instruction she received as

"pop religion." The church's social teaching was not presented, and she and her classmates looked on the teaching about sex as a sick joke.

Mary's theological and scriptural education was essentially begun at college where she majored in Religious Studies. Upon graduation in 1979, she sought and found work in the new diocesan office of Peace and Justice. Today being "Catholic" for Mary is still part of a family and cultural heritage, but beyond that it represents a personal choice and commitment. She finds hope in the church's social message, the means of deepening the spiritual dimension of her life in the church's resources, and support in Catholic friends who are about the same thing: building the kingdom. These same friends can share the inevitable frustrations that attend the effort.

Furthering her own education on social justice issues and sharing the growing knowledge is one of the most satisfying and challenging aspects of her present job. A woman of Hispanic/Chinese background she feels she brings a special sensitivity and a valuable viewpoint to the work of the office, and that in many ways her very presence there can enable others, clergy and lay, to come to a new understanding of church. She had hoped to be more directly involved in women's issues as an aspect of social justice, but finds that being a diocesan employee places certain restrictions in this area. The compromise required by the dichotomy between her personal views and official church practice or teaching (e.g. on the question of women's ordination) is, indeed, one of the constraints of working in a diocesan office.

Mary's views on women and her own lifestyle have been profoundly influenced by the women's movement. "Feminists who risked things, changed their conception of what it means to be a woman, uncovered lies and in the process gave up certain securities," she says, "brought me to a new and freeing idea of myself as woman." Acquaintance with women thinkers brought her to a realization that the lives of women, whose existence revolved around men, were often narrow and confined. From the idea that her true fulfillment and meaning as woman would come only through a man, Mary has moved to clear-eyed belief that women can be healthy, wealthy, wise and whole while emotionally, financially and socially independent of men.

The freeing of women from positions of dependency and from a self-image as helper and satellite would, in Mary's opinion, have important repercussions in the church. The presence of women as true ministers on a par with men in the church would bring new vibrancy to its mission and would encourage women who have left to come back, be healed, participate once more in the church's sacramental life, and find new understanding and a wider scope for their own gifts.

As it is, many women and Mary herself find large portions of the all-male clergy wanting in terms of leadership and prophetic witness. The "sacred brotherhood" appears to be threatened by lay people, and especially by women, and more especially by single women. Pronouncements from Rome and from American pulpits reveal a stubborn and sad lack of understanding of today's women. While Mary agrees, for instance, with the anti-abortion stance of the church, she regrets the failure of churchmen to deal adequately with the questions of rape, teenage sexuality, and the economic circumstance of women in our society. The reiteration of the fact that life is sacred and that a fetus is a stage of human life should be combined with a serious consideration of why women seek abortions and with practical ways of supporting them.

While the greater visibility and influence of women at all levels of church ministry and decision-making is a goal of first importance, Mary concurs with those women who stress that we must change rather than perpetuate present patterns of wielding power, bringing with us to all positions gifts of life, nourishment, and renewal.

We must also address more directly and profoundly questions concerning sexuality and women in the church, whether single, married or professed religious. Mary feels that the general impression of women connected with the work of the church is that they are, at best, asexual and at worst, frigid and unfeeling.

In Mary Yu we have an example of a young woman who recognizes the church's caution, clericalism, and inconsistencies, but who looks to it for a steady pursuit of the truth and who is willing, herself, to join in that quest. She finds in the church a community struggling to keep alive the principles of the Gospel, and people who, like her, are striving to live more simply and to become more prayerful. Keenly aware of the social, psychological and economic disabilities that can hinder minority women, Mary herself presents to the world a person of unmistakable leadership ability with mind and spirit refreshingly honest, forward-looking, and whole.

MOLLY BURKE: MOTHER, WIFE, AND SCHOLAR

Molly (Quinn) Burke grew up as a "professional" Catholic in the Anglo-Saxon Protestant town of Dover, Massachusetts. Her mother taught her the essentials of the faith, and it was in family circles that she came gradually to appreciate the advantage that the few Catholic families held over their neighbors: moral superiority. "Let the prosperous lawyer ride by in his Cadillac to rendezvous with his mistress; my mother was bringing beef stew to the old, sick woman on the corner of the block! We Catholics might be less prosperous in the eyes of the world; we were surely more just in the eyes of God," she says recalling her youthful assessment of her Catholic identity.

Secure in this knowledge, Molly went from public grade school to a Catholic high school, and from the notion that church was family to one that the church was the Sisters of St. Joseph. At their command, she dutifully memorized church history and uncritically absorbed the contents of one religious textbook a year.

At this point Molly's moral beliefs were those taught by the church, and her behavior was modified by what she was prepared to report in confession. Her social and political beliefs were, by and large, those of the Democratic party. She shared the anti-Vietnam convictions of her generation, but did not cease to be responsive to authority figures and did not join the ranks of insurgents.

In her senior year at Boston College, Molly was introduced to situation ethics and began to recognize options other than those dictated by Catholic practice as morally acceptable. Less righteous in her judgments and more tolerant of differences, she nevertheless freely chose the church's moral sanctions and guidelines for herself. In the wake of the insistent questioning that swept the church in the 70's, however, Molly began to look upon the church with more critical eyes. What she had once seen as a humane institution now often appeared misguided. Certain church rules failed to take into account the facts of real-life situations, and imposed harsh judgment or unreasonable burdens.

Now, as a mother of three sons, the eldest of whom is a first grader in a parochial school, Molly sees herself as Catholic mostly in virtue of being a parent. She attributes her continuing conviction in part to her husband, Ed, a well-read and very self-aware Catholic.

Her hopes for her children are that they will grow

into the conviction that being Catholic means living out Christ's teaching. For the moment, her first grader is caught up in the mysteries of the sacramental system and learning prayers by heart, and seems to see God as a heavenly score-keeper. She hopes to be able eventually to deepen in him and all of her children a sense of the human connections in the Christian community and a sense of the meaning of spiritual journey.

The sense of marriage as sacrament, spouses as the source of one another's salvation, and of the necessity for a heavy personal investment in family are clearly strong convictions and values of highest priority with Molly Burke. But her energies have always been expended in circles beyond the family.

As a young mother she worked as Director of Housing and Dean of Students in Catholic colleges. She is presently working for a Ph.D. in higher education administration at Northwestern University, and plans eventually to work in a Catholic college or university again. Like many women who are juggling the responsibilities and demands of marriage, motherhood, and study or work, Molly often feels overwhelmed. The combination would be impossible were it not for the fact that her husband supports her in the goals she has set for herself, and translates that support into the practical form of sharing housework, cooking, and the care of the children. Even then, the attempt to combine professional goals and domestic duties takes its emotional toll. "When I'm home, I feel guilty about not working at the dissertation; when I'm at the University, I feel guilty about home." The attitude of the Catholic church and clergy doesn't help. Rather than insisting on principles that would facilitate the work of women outside the home: equal pay, equal access to promotion, and the need for a family to share domestic labor, papal and clerical statements often reinforce the guilt and depict the goals of married women with careers as contradictory. "The church," says Molly, "doesn't even *pretend* to be understanding of women's position." Women, and indeed all church members, need more encouragement and less admonishment.

At the moment, Molly feels overextended and finds ample scope for service and ministry close to home. Ministry for Molly means what she does every day for her family ("though I don't want to make them my score card with God!"), and will include later her work in a Catholic university or college. Still, she is intrigued by the call to greater simplicity and service to the poor that Dorothy Day's life presents. The Catholic Worker movement represents for her what is best in the Catholic tradition and she finds in it a challenge to her whole lifestyle. Those who have devoted themselves to the alleviation of social injustice are the ones who open her mind and her horizon, who recall her to a sense of prayer, of true values, of what is ultimately important.

What changes would Molly Burke like to see in Mother Church? "I would like to have more available the tools to deal with the tension between belief and unbelief and the means of deepening my spiritual life." The homilies she hears deal too often with issues such as the need for vocations, alcoholism, the missionary church or with superficial suggestions for getting ready for church feasts. She would like to see women more visible and clearly equal in the church's ministry, and feels the church will be weakened if it continues to exclude women from certain positions. Women themselves need not be hindered by present restrictions, however, and she hopes that the church's best people will work where they can do so freely and will not be consumed in a struggle or a hopeless cause. "But I know the church will be deprived if it continues in the vein of the oppression of women."

Molly Burke serves to represent the Catholic mother of the 80's whose life and interests are home-centered, yes, but whose intellectual and professional strivings lead her to look beyond "Kinder und Küche." She is comfortable in the church, and seems to conform easily to the rules of membership. She respects the church's stability, and looks to it as one of the socializing factors which will make of her children value-oriented persons—Christians for whom Easter means more than bunnies.

Molly Burke and the educated, reflective women like her are not at a loss to indicate where the institutional church might better serve them, but they look to it for a steady reminder of the New Testament message and of the primacy of spiritual over material values.

JOAN O'SHEA: CHAPLAIN, MEDICAL CENTER

Although she was baptized into the church in 1930, Joan O'Shea dates her birth as a self-aware Catholic from 1962 when she was studying in Rome. Here, studying theology, in contact with a broader range of people than ever before, and close to the day-by-day work of Vatican Council II, she became acutely aware of her Catholic identity and of the need to examine what she had heretofore quite blindly accepted. The examination extended to the meaning of authority in the church, to the relationship between the various Christian churches, to the realities of being woman in the church, and to the mythology and mystique of the religious life to which she was committed.

Others going through this same exercise felt betrayed and angry; angry at the waste of years spent in obedience to meaningless rules and restrictions; angry at the repression of emotion and sexuality which religious life imposed; angry at the sacrifice of person to organization; angry at the slowness with which all of this was changed. Joan's primary response was one of excitement and gratitude to be alive in times that were moving. She wonders now, with a laugh, if this might be because of a need to minimize or suppress the negative and unpleasant, or if it might stem from a sense of personal freedom that had characterized earlier choices—personal freedom and good sense that had been enhanced rather than hampered in a Catholic high school education with the Sinsinawa Dominicans whom she eventually joined.

Joan has brought her gifts to a number of different ministries: first-grade teaching, college teaching and administration, and, most recently, hospital chaplaincy. Joan chose to train and to work as a hospital chaplain, at first, in non-sectarian or Lutheran hospitals. She experienced greater freedom in these settings, and, she says, "There was no need to face the reluctance of Catholics—clergy or laity—to change." The experience of ministering to and being ministered to by Lutherans, Episcopalians, and Methodists was enriching. Joining the staff of a Catholic hospital, St. Joseph's in South Bend, Indiana, in 1981, represented a certain risk. But she has found there the same affirmation and respect, both personally and professionally, that she enjoyed in more ecumemical settings. Her colleagues accept her as a co-equal minister. "Still," she says, "I have a strange feeling of being taken for granted as a sister." And it's a bit discouraging to have to go the rounds again about not wearing a habit. She describes a typical enounter:

Joan: "Hello, I'm Sister Joan O'Shea."

Patient (indignantly): "How would I ever *know* you're a sister?"

Joan (patiently and looking her right in the eye): "I just *told* you."

Has being a woman closed doors to her as hospital chaplain? Joan resents the fact that as a woman she can be certified as pastoral associate but not as chaplain by the National Association of Catholic Chaplains. The title chaplain is reserved for the ordained. A resolution to bury the distinction in titles was proposed two years ago, but the membership voted the motion down. Being unordained also limits job opportunities to a certain extent, and, more fundamentally, the fact that sacramental ministry is closed to her on the basis of sex leads, on the theoretical level, to feelings of anger and diminishment. On the experiential level, however, there are too many other ways of ministering open to her for Joan to focus on the question of closed doors. She preaches, and does so in the manner of one who has taken time with the Word, examined it from new angles, and woven it into her own existence. She helps sensitize hospital staff, nurses and physicians, to the spiritual needs of patients and suggests ways of meeting them. She has worked with cancer patients and their families, and in pain rehabilitation centers. She consults, lectures and teaches. And she talks with, and prays with, numerous patients who can be themselves in her presence: weak and afraid, perhaps, or resentful, or lonely, or needing to be reconciled. In situations where both patients and their families are particularly vulnerable, Joan manages to avoid easy cliches or phrases of hollow piety. She listens, she stays with, she sees, she interprets, and slowly enables others to hope, or pray, or take heart, or be comforted.

Joan is keenly aware of the need to find ways to help lay people, nurses, managerial staff and parish members exercise their right and call to minister. She likes to recall a patient who at first complained that no one (read "priest") from the church had come to visit her, but upon reflection was satisfied that the church had, indeed, been present in a visit of her neighbor. Joan fosters this growing recognition that the church is all of us, and that we are all ministers. It has an obvious practical advantage in a time when priests and religious are at a premium, but at a deeper level conforms to the theological truth of the priesthood of all.

As a woman who has been touched by the women's movement, Joan also brings to the staff a sensitivity to the issues that have been raised by feminists in the last two decades. The questions of women's rights in the field of medicine, of inclusive language in services provided by the chaplaincy, of different attitudes toward men and women patients, of different attitudes of patients toward male, ordained chaplains and female, lay chaplains can be examined in much greater depth when probed by a staff which includes women and men, ordained and unordained. Joan sees these particular questions as a small part of the awakening of women that has occurred in the last two decades. She sees the feminist movement as a religious and spiritual event, proof that "God's creation is a continuing phenomenon." Through it, "God is calling to life what was dormant in women," she says.

Since the early 1960's then, Joan has had to re-choose or reject the values associated with vowed life, and has become increasingly conscious of the meaning of being woman in a male-dominated church or world. The pain involved in this process is not to be compared with the freedom won, the sense of new possibilities, and the joy at being alive at such a time. What lies ahead? For Joan, personally, growth in the future will mean becoming more prayerful. "I don't believe in a God who magically makes changes at my request," she says, "but I would like more often simply to place before God the people and situations that I cannot touch, that no one can touch, and pray that a communion can be realized between God and those for whom I pray." And growth will mean freeing herself from the work-achievement-success compulsion that has propelled her since childhood. "It will mean treasuring and deepening friendships, becoming more aware of the circle which is turning, and preparing for the next phase of my life: old age." Still in an active and vital middle-age, Joan seeks to meld activity and surrender, and to prepare for the day when she can say (and it isn't easy for her to say it even now in remote anticipation) "If you want my life today, I'm ready." Meanwhile, she wants above all to be unashamed to share her unfinished and rich self.

Here, then, are seven women in the American Catholic church who represent various backgrounds and ages, who work in the suburbs and inner city, who are single, married, or vowed religious. In long interviews with each of them, I often thought *here* is the salt of the earth, *here* is the church alive and well.

Direct, self-aware, honest, and more and more comfortable with their own authority, they are less concerned with official church pronouncements than they are with the truth of their own experience (and the experience of those with whom and for whom they work) read in the light of Christian faith.

Aware of discrimination against women in the church, and intent on eliminating it, they are, nevertheless, neither crippled nor immobilized by it. And conscious of the failures of the institutional church in many cases, they nevertheless look to the church as people, to the church as tradition and milieu, to give meaning and direction to their lives and to offer the world a constant witness to the power of love and spirit and truth over the forces of hatred, greed, and destruction.

Chapter Two

SEX AND IDENTITY
IN AND OUT OF
MARRIAGE:
PART ONE

Questions of Value

THE next two chapters cover a wide range of issues involving identity and human sexuality in and out of marriage, especially as these issues touch the lives of Catholic women. The structures, with their rules and regulations, which have shaped and governed women's lives as wives, divorcees, singles, or nuns have been seriously questioned and re-formed since Vatican II. Some read in the changes a crisis of authority and a distressing breakdown of Catholic values. But behind the questions, the debate, and even the rebellion, lies a desire not to overthrow or dilute values but to search freely for a new expression of them in structures better-suited to today's world.

Can the church accommodate this search? The church conceived of as a community of being, a community in process, is ideally suited to do so.[1] In such a community, the role of authority is not to protect or prevent mistakes, to legislate in minute detail, to sniff out and condemn deviations, but to motivate, inspire, and provide a living example of the ideal. Leaders articulate values and provide vision which is based on the experience of the members of the community. Freedom, maturity, and responsible decision-making are at home in this atmosphere. Those who make mistakes or fail are not excommunicated, but are asked, "What have you learned? How can we help you into the next step?"

These considerations are relevant to the questions pursued in the next two chapters. Women look for and welcome a reiteration of the values of sexual responsibility, the sacredness of person and of life, and the permanency of marriage: all absolutes on the level of moral discussion. They look for greater freedom of expression of these values on the level of moral decision, and on the level of the social structures which embody them.

The Search For Wholeness

Women have carried the burden of myth, misconception and guilt which overlies their sexual identity into this eighth decade of the twentieth century. In 1982 it is still a challenge for a woman to achieve at once a firm sense of self as an autonomous individual, and the fullness of her sexual potential through the various stages of her life. Many of the women who answered my questionnaire attribute their difficulty in attaining this integration in great part to the teaching of the Catholic church.

The tendency to define women solely in terms of

their reproductive capacity and their relationships is
not, of course, confined to the church. Page Smith,
an American historian, could write as late as 1975,
"Unless women respect this order—childhood,
girlhood, wifehood, motherhood, and grandmotherhood—they will end up unhappy wayfarers in
the valley of dolls."[2] Women have become acutely
conscious, however, that the question of personal
identity is *not* solved by opting for wifehood,
motherhood and grandmotherhood. These roles cannot bear the weight of women's identity.[3] Quotations
based on the same assumptions as Smith's could be
multiplied indefinitely in literature from various
fields, so we can readily concede that the church
does not bear sole responsibility for whatever fear,
guilt, or self-splintering mark women in their search
for personhood and sexual fulfillment. Nonetheless,
most Catholic women find that church teaching has
been a significant factor in their concept of
themselves as sexual beings.

Sixty women answered the question "How has
church teaching on sexuality affected your life?"
These women, in their late 20's to 60's, and from
various parts of the United States, were single, married, or members of religious congregations. Most
are practicing Catholics, although some, like
Theodora Jankowski (Utica, NY) and Suzanne Oster-
busch (Downers Grove, IL), have left the church
primarily because of the widening gap between their
personal experience and intellectual conviction in
regard to female sexuality and the church's official

stance on questions related to it. The former writes:

> As a guilt-ridden high school student I judiciously
> confessed all the "evil" thoughts I had about
> sex...Now all I can do is laugh at the church's out-
> moded antics regarding it. The church would deny
> me one of my vital, biological, emotional necessities
> as a human being simply because I am not married.
> This whole area, I find, is one of the most
> hypocritical in the church.

Another single young woman, Kathleen F. Kelly of
Chicago, struggles with the discrepancy between her
sexual behaviour, which she sees as responsible, and
church teaching on pre-marital sex and birth control—a discrepancy which, she says, raises questions
for her about her Roman Catholic identity.

In general, however, the women answering this
question were firm in their identity as Catholics.
Eighteen percent answered that the church's
teaching and positions on questions related to sex
had had a positive effect on their lives whether in
convincing them that hedonistic sexuality doesn't
work, or in equipping them with stricter morals than
the younger generation manifests. Kathleen Miller of
Mount Prospect, Illinois, observed that the nuns who
taught her (from 1952 to 1968) were not warped, and
she continued, "Fidelity to the marriage covenant
has given my husband and me freedom we never an-
ticipated—freedom of honesty and intimacy,
freedom of friendship with others." Marie Ponsot of
New York credits church teaching for keeping her a

virgin till she was nineteen and had earned her degree, and then for equipping her with the liberating idea that her own conscience was the ultimate arbiter of her sexual mores.

Thirty percent responded that church teaching on sex-related matters has had little or no effect because they learned early to rely on their own consciences, judging church teaching to be at best unrealistic, and at worst nonsense. Sunny Lopez, a convert of five years, describes herself as constantly in the process of discerning what to accept and what to reject.

Fifty-three percent of respondents described the effect on them of church teaching and attitudes as negative. Recurrent themes in their answers were the late acceptance of their sexuality, sometimes delayed until their late 30's after having borne several children, fear and ignorance of sex, guilt, and shame. "The church taught me to beware of my ideas and to be ashamed of my dreams," writes 53 year old Rosemary Dixon. Two suburban mothers with large families accepted the church's teaching on birth control, like so many of their contemporaries in the 50's, and did not anticipate the strain and enormous difficulties in having children too close together. "I had neither the time nor energy to do a decent job raising them," says Barbara Ross. Mary Jo Weaver, professor in the Religious Studies Department at Indiana University, rejected marriage precisely because of the church's position that "marriage meant tons of kids as God's inexorable will for marrying in the first place." A young woman in

Minneapolis associates church teaching on sexual
matters more closely with her self-identity than with
her actual sexual behavior: "I grew up believing that
I was flawed! It is *only* from my bonding with other
women and much counseling that I reversed that
self-image."

Among Catholic women in the 80's there is
generally a tendency toward coming to terms with
their sexuality, exercising personal judgment in what
concerns their sexual behavior, and developing confidence in themselves as persons who transcend
roles. If they still look to the church for help in forming a right conscience, most would agree with Marie
Ponsot, one of *Commonweal's* poetry editors, that the
church would do well to let much of its regulatory
function lapse. She suggests, "Let the church bend
its teaching to the discovery of what we all need to be
or become more humanely human, less harmful,
more full of charity, more prolific of acts of hope,
and more capable of worship together."

The Changing Family

Church and society presented, until recently, a
model of the family in which roles were well-defined
and unequal. Husbands and fathers were the bread-
winners, the protectors, the ultimate decision-
makers and the heads of households. Wives and
mothers were economic dependents, homemakers,
and servants of husbands and children alike.
Children had filial duties, but few rights. Economic

conditions, greater access to higher education, the adoption of birth control methods, and the transformation in consciousness effected by the women's movement have converged to call this model into question, if not to render it obsolete. A countermovement gaining strength in the charismatic renewal insists on the God-given order of the traditional model, however, and struggles to maintain it.

Whether one mourns or welcomes the changes taking place in the American family, it is no longer possible to ignore them. One of the most notable changes, and the one which has gained wide social acceptance is the phenomenon of the working mother. From 1960 to 1979 the percentage of married women, with husband present and with children from ages 6 to 17, who participated in the labor force, rose from 39 to 59 percent. During the same period the percentage of working women with children under six rose from 18.6 to 43.2 percent.[4] Statisticians and trend predictors expect the number of families in which both parents work to leap to 80 percent by 1990.

Other trends which have changed the nature of the American family are the rising divorce rate, the growing practice of couples living together without marrying, and the increasing number of families headed by one parent, usually a woman. These trends are documented in the statistics recently published by the U.S. Census Bureau. From 1970 to 1980 these figures indicate rises of 65 percent in divorces granted, of 157.4 percent in unmarried

couples, and of 40.1 percent in one-parent families.
So profound and widespread is the transformation
in family patterns brought about by rapid
technological and scientific development or by
changing cultural norms that some, in alarm, ask
whether the family, and therefore the civilization of
which it is the basic cell, is not in grave danger of
dissolution. The fact is, however, that there has
never been a definition of family which adequately
covered the wide array of social structures which
might conceivably be covered by that term. Furthermore, the family has always been in flux and has ever
proved adaptable to the circumstances imposed by
different times and different environments.[5]

This realization can serve to temper the distress of
those who might otherwise view current changes in
family patterns as stages in the slow but certain
death of civilization as we have known it. The fact
remains, however, that change in our own time has
been particularly rapid and that, while new options
have proved liberating in many respects, the sudden
disappearance of old securities has been a source of
pain and confusion for many. Women's work outside
the home is a case in point.

Married Women And Work

For married women, the question of work has been
a central one in the tension between new freedoms
and possibilities and old expectations and obligations. Young and young middle-aged women ex-

perience a pull between the desire to begin or continue work in a job or professional field and the
demands of home-making and child-rearing. Even if
they prefer the work involved in being mother and
wife, they realize that often couples do not live happily ever after, and that their acquisition and exercise of professional skills could be crucial in the case
of divorce or early widowhood. And even if they
could be secure in the knowledge of remaining happily married into old age, more and more women
seek the personal fulfillment, the contact with a
wider world of productive adults, and the sense of
worth and belonging which work outside the home
provides. From another point of view, whether they
find it fulfilling or not, work has become an
economic necessity for most married women. Most
of them find that the problems that arise in a family
where both spouses work outside the home have not
been squarely faced, let alone solved.

Pope John Paul II addresses the question of women
and work in his recent encyclical "Laborem Exercens." It will be worthwhile to examine this document to see to what extent the hierarchical church
appreciates the modern Catholic mother's aspirations and frustrations in regard to her work both
within and without the home.

In his encyclical, John Paul II demonstrates some
sensitivity to the issues of discrimination and the
conflicting demands of work at home and in the
marketplace. At four points in his text he singles out
women, and he is justified in so doing to the extent

that women's experience of the world of work is different from that of men. However, treating women as a special category has the unfortunate effect of grouping all women together on the unique basis of gender; an approach that seems to rest on the assumption that the fact of being women predominates over all individual variations. This would be unthinkable, of course, for men. Furthermore, it reinforces the suspicion that in the rest of the encyclical his remarks refer, not to human work, but to the work of males. The consistent use of the pseudo-generic "man" throughout the translation does nothing to dispel this suspicion.

John Paul II's perception (one he shares with large segments of the hierarchy and of men at large) of men as individuals and of women as an unindividuated group becomes explicit in the following passage:

> The books of the Old Testament contain main [sic] references to human work and to the individual professions exercised by man: for example, the doctor, the pharmacist, the craftsman or artist, the blacksmith—we could apply these words to today's foundry workers—the potter, the farmer, the scholar, the sailor, the builder, the musician, the shepherd, and the fisherman.

> The words of praise for the work of women are well known. In his parables on the kingdom of God, Jesus Christ constantly refers to human work: that of the shepherd, the farmer, the doctor, the sower, the

householder, the servant, the steward, the fisherman, the merchant, the laborer. *He also speaks of the various forms of women's work* [emphasis mine]. He compares the apostolate to the manual work of harvesters or fishermen. He refers to the work of scholars too.[6]

To indicate the nature of "women's work" John Paul II refers to two New Testament passages: Matthew 13:33 where the kingdom of heaven is compared to a woman who takes yeast and mixes it with flour, and Luke 15:8-9 in which a woman sweeps her house in search of a lost coin. Thus, he equates "women's work" with household tasks, and fails to recognize the existence of women among doctors, pharmacists, artists, farmers, and musicians. He furthermore equates human work with the work of males, as indicated by the addition of the sentence in italics. We are once again confronted with a document which stereotypes male and female occupations.

It is in the section entitled "Wages and other Social Benefits" that the Pope specifically takes up the question of mothers and work. We might note in passing that he seems to equate being woman with being mother. He notes in this section that:

Just remuneration for the work of an adult who is responsible for a family means remuneration which will suffice for establishing and properly maintaining a family and for providing security for its future. Such remuneration can be given either through what is called a family wage—that is, a single salary given

to the head of the family for his work, sufficient for
the needs of the family without the other spouse having to take up gainful employment outside the
home—or through other social measures such as
family allowances or grants to mothers devoting
themselves exclusively to their families.[7]

A family wage or family allowances or grants to
mothers are ways of indirectly recognizing the contribution of women whose work in the home has a
market value readily determined by the current costs
of hiring a cook, housecleaner, laundress, gardener,
and babysitter. Women who would choose to remain
at home if it were economically feasible would surely
welcome such solutions. And most women will agree
with Patricia Somers Cronin who remarked, "John
Paul II was right to salute mothers who stay home."
She is the mother of six and stayed home until last
summer when she went back to work as an editor
and found it exhilarating. Still she remarks, "I could
see the danger for a young woman." She continues,
"I think the church has not faced up to the woman
with talent who marries. . . . This whole area needs
re-thinking."

Her remarks reflect a certain tension: work outside
domestic confines is exhilarating—but perhaps
dangerous for a young woman—yet the church
should face up to the questions posed by talented
young married women as they consider their options
and try to reconcile their career aspirations with the
demands of home.

Another woman commenting on church teaching

on attitudes about women and work writes, "The church continues to send out a subliminal message that a woman's place is in the home." Bonnie Williams agrees and continues: "This stance is the most universally archaic. So many families need mothers to work that this attitude. . . is just ignored. Though I ignore the church's attitude on working women I wish I could find comfort there."

In fact, the encyclical on work, as well as the "Apostolic Exhortation on the Family," acknowledges that women's role in society is not exclusively that of wife and mother, that women should have equal access with men to public functions, and that women in fact work in nearly every sector of life. But the dominant note is that it is a pity that women are compelled to work outside the home, and the call is for society to develop conditions favoring work in the home.[8]

John Paul II fails utterly to take into account the growing number of married women who are searching, not for ways to stay at home with subsidies, but for ways to become economically independent through work outside the home. While the Pope emphasizes the care and education of children as the *mother's* primary role, these women stress the fact that parents share these duties and that the whole family should share the work of maintaining the home. John Paul II's reference to women "abandoning what is specific to them," and his admonition that labor should be structured in such a way that women's advancement not be at the expense of the family, suggest that women have a monopoly on child-rearing and housework. The question of family and the work of women is far from being solved by the suggestion that work should be structured in such a way that women can work in the marketplace *and* care for their children *and* do the cooking *and* do the housework. The challenge is to structure work in such a way that women and men together can care for and educate their children, maintain a home, and share the benefits and the boredom, perhaps, of work outside the home.

Equality and economic opportunities for women should not be viewed primarily as threats to the family, but as goals to be achieved. If women's personal and economic freedom must not be pursued at the expense of the family, neither must family welfare be bought at the price of women's sacrifice of professional training, career goals, leisure, or mental health. Younger couples appear to be working out satisfactory solutions, and some companies are beginning to take into account the fact that, in many cases, both spouses have jobs or careers as well as family obligations. It nevertheless remains for families themselves and for the church and other public and private institutions to seek imaginative ways, not to tie women more firmly to domestic duties by paying them to perform them, but ways to assure that the normal avenues of human development are open equally to women and men. The care and education of children is of utmost importance, but the responsibility is parental and not maternal.

Once all the implications of this are grasped, it becomes meaningless to compare the value of women's maternal role with their public role, as John Paul II does in "The Apostolic Exhortation on the Family." The equal dignity and responsibility of men and women to which he refers will be truly realized in marriage only when each spouse takes it for granted that both will assume work in the home and in rearing children as well as "breadwinning" labor.

Until this is the case, John Paul II's insistence that work in the home and in the rearing of children (which he assigns to women) be recognized and respected for its irreplaceable value will ring false. Let his reminder go out with another: that men and women share these respected tasks. Let us once and for all cease typing men and women's work, protesting loudly that the work which falls to women's lot is just as desirable and valuable as that reserved to men.

An excellent example of such stereotyping is furnished by the advice given by the fathers of Notre Dame in their *Religious Bulletin* of the 40's. They counseled their students to domesticate their fiancées even before marriage, lest they, as husbands, get stuck with the dishes.[9] The advice is an unwitting illustration of Simone de Beauvoir's trenchant remark that women are given a vocation of motherhood to get them to do the dishes. Her point was that the choice to give birth is clearly distinct from a choice to be mainly responsible for housework. Indeed, de Beauvoir believes that all women should find employment in the marketplace, and should not have the choice of staying at home.

This choice, in practice approved only for women, has the effect of creating an economically dependent social group which constitutes at the same time a pool of cheap labor. Women who leave the labor market suffer severe handicaps when later, divorced, widowed, or forced to augment family income, they return to it. The assumption of employers that women will leave work when they decide to have children prejudices their willingness to invest in their training or to promote them at the same pace as men. Women themselves set their sights lower than men do, being conditioned to think that they will be taken care of once married.

All women suffer, then, for the erratic patterns of women in the work force—patterns reinforced by the idea that women should have the choice of working or remaining at home, a choice never seriously offered to men. This choice might appear a luxury; it is actually a liability. It helps explain the widespread poverty of women as a social group.

Wages For Housewives?

The "solution" of paying women for work in the home appeals to some women. Phyllis Chesler and Emily Jane Goodman recognize that this would keep women where they already are, namely at home, but favor wages for housewives because payment could provide security and financial liquidity.[10] They do not see financial payment as an ultimate answer, but suggest that a housewives' union would give these women more control over their lives.

This solution does not address the basic inequalities between men and women in relation to work. If there is to be payment for home labor, it should be conceived, *not* as wages for housewives, but as recompense for housework, whether done by men or women. But in fact it is hardly conceivable that men would take the option... respectable, dignified, and worthy as full-time child-rearing and housework is. And why not? Perhaps because the economic and psychological cost would be too great?

This leads us back to the solution of equal sharing by both spouses of the work of raising a family. Both will assume child-rearing and household tasks as unpaid duties, and both will meet the financial needs of the family through work in the marketplace. This option admittedly sidesteps the question of child care, and it is this problem that family, church, and state must approach creatively. On the positive side, however, it eliminates problems raised by attempting to put a dollar value on the emotional investment and the practical tasks involved in creating a home which are properly the province of both spouses.

Catholic women are perhaps more prone than others to feel guilty if they begin to question the assumption that women should shoulder the burden of home-making virtually alone, that they should embrace self-annihilation and self-sacrifice for the good of the family. Equally, they tend to feel culpable if

they begin to resent vicarious financial rewards
(their husband's pay) or vicarious success (their husband's or children's achievements).

The church in its concern for family life must be
careful not to reinforce that guilt. Genuine concern
for the family must include concern for the healthy
personhood of wives and mothers. In practice this
will mean supporting them as they search for ways
out of economic exploitation in and out of the home,
and as they struggle to integrate career and family. It
will mean affirming them, not only in the non-
threatening and underpaid professions traditionally
followed by women, but in the new and unexpected
ones, justly recompensed, whether in business or in
the church itself. It will mean seeing and ap-
preciating them not only as propagators of the
human race and irreplaceable mainstays of the family. It will mean recognizing the validity and en-
couraging the fulfillment of their personal educational and career goals. It will mean extending to
them, in short, what has always and unconsciously
been afforded men.

Divorce and Remarriage

After a period of shock and denial in the 60's,
Catholics have come to terms with the fact that
divorce has become as common in our ranks as in
the population at large. And in the population at
large, the national divorce rate increased 82 percent
between 1963 and 1972. In 1973 there was roughly

one divorce for 2.5 marriages. From 1970 to 1980 the U.S. Census Bureau notes an increase of 65.3 percent in the number of divorces granted; the number jumped from 708,000 in 1970, to 1,170,000 in 1980.

At first condemnatory and punitive toward its members whose marriages had "failed," both the official church and church members, in most cases, now offer them sustained friendship, psychological and emotional support, and full inclusion in the life of the parish. In her response to the questions I addressed to the divorced woman, "Have you found support in church related associations?" and "What part did your faith or church membership play in your experience of going through a divorce, or of being divorced?," Mary Jean Argento, divorced and remarried, speaks for increasing numbers of recently divorced Catholic women:

> My relation to the church has not changed since my divorce. My pastor continues to be supportive to us both and we have experienced no rejection in this area. My first counselor was a priest-psychologist. He gave me strength and made sense throughout the turmoil. Other priests I've sought out were equally supportive and stressed following my conscience throughout the experience.

Another woman cites a peer-group, SWORD (Separated, Widowed, or Divorced Catholics) as particularly helpful, and remarks that her faith and church membership made bearable the whole experience. "My own stereotypes of the 'divorced' were carryovers from childhood which I had to overcome," she observes.

Although both of these women have experienced their church membership as a positive dimension in the painful process which ended in the dissolution of their marriages, Mary Jean Argento is among those who, according to John Paul II, must not be admitted to the eucharist because her "state and condition of life objectively contradict that union of love between Christ and the church which is signified and effected by the eucharist."[11] She is in this unhappy condition because, for reasons unknown to her, the marriage tribunal of Chicago refused her an annulment. Paradoxically, her experience of her second marriage is that it is an authentic sign of the union between Christ and the church, while her first had become a contradiction.

She is, at least, not excommunicated. In 1977 the United States Bishops' Committee for Canonical Affairs recommended to the Holy See the removal of the penalty of excommunication from divorced American Catholics who remarried, a penalty dating back to the III Plenary Council of Baltimore (1884). The official removal of this penalty accorded with the common opinion of canonists that it no longer applied. The Bishops were careful to underline the fact, however, that the church did not consider civil marriages after divorce valid, and that Catholics entering them were not to be permitted to participate in the eucharist. Church annulment remains the only means of entering a valid second marriage.

The continued exclusion of Catholics who divorce and remarry in a civil ceremony from what has always been the sign of full membership in the Catholic community, namely the receiving of the eucharist, sign and symbol of Christian reconciliation and unity, stems, of course, from concern that were they to join the community at the eucharistic table, the force of the church's teaching about the indissolubility of marriage would be diluted. This in spite of the fact that most Catholics are expressing their continued belief in the permanence of marriage while profoundly questioning the wisdom, and even the right, of the hierarchy in their continued refusal of the church's central sacrament to those who have been unable to obtain annulments, or perhaps even to those who judge the whole tribunal procedure as meaningless and unnecessary.

This is expressed clearly in the working paper on the family which was prepared at the United States Bishops' Conference on Liberty and Justice for All for the American Bicentennial:

> Nowhere in the testimony is there any suggestion that the church back off the clear call of the Lord to permanence and fidelity in marriage....Rather, people call for a kind of pastoral solicitude which would see the church community enter into the pain of divorce and offer healing and new life. They want those whose marriages have ended not to be punished for failure for which they are often not responsible; they want to see them surrounded with love and acceptance, even should they choose to marry

again...The divorced and remarried themselves are
asking the church to be present to this perilous process and to offer validation to their often lonely,
painful decisions. They crave the approval of the
Catholic community...their only spiritual home,
and they long for that full Catholic life which only
sharing at the Eucharistic table permits.[12]

The Good Conscience Solution has been the
answer of many to this problem. The solution no
longer enjoys public, diocesan approbation, but it is
still applied privately by priests and lay people. It
provides that couples who are sincerely convinced
that the prior marriage of one or both of them was in-
valid, although this could not be proven in a marriage tribunal, and that their second marriage is a
true one, are indeed validly married and fully in communion with the church. The advantages and disad-
vantages of this approach are discussed by Stephen J.
Kelleher in his book on divorce and remarriage.[13] He
sees the solution as superior to the tribunal process,
but concludes that it is often confusing and uncer-
tain since couples are rarely able to say with cer-
titude whether or why their first marriages never
truly existed. Monsignor Kelleher investigates the
whole question of divorce and remarriage real-
istically, honestly, and humanely. With a doctorate
in canon law, and long years of experience with the
Marriage Tribunal of the Archdiocese of New York,
he cannot be accused of failing to appreciate the
legal, theological, or social implications of divorce

and remarriage within the church. With years of study and experience behind him, he proposes the "Welcome Home" solution to the problem of the intolerable marriage. Quite simply, this solution recognizes that once a marriage has become irrevocably intolerable, once it has died, each party has a right to divorce, to marry a second time, and to be fully accepted in the religious community of his or her choice. They would seek guidance and counsel, but would make the decisions themselves. Catholics would be welcomed at the eucharist, and have every right to participate in all of the activities of the church. They would be at home in the church. Those only would be excluded who showed a blatant disregard for the basic values of marriage. He suggests further that the second marriage ordinarily be blessed publicly by the church and the couple welcomed by a genuinely Christian community.[14]

This generous, pastoral "Welcome Home" solution and this insistence on a couple's exercise of conscience, accords well with the reflection of a Catholic woman who has gone through separation, divorce, annulment, and single parenthood. She writes:

I believe marriage should be forever. However, when one party walks away from wife and family, I have to question the validity of the initial vows. Also, there has to be a place for those left behind who cannot face a whole (today very much *longer*) lifetime alone. I have seen women driven to seek spouses for financial reasons and for a father for their children, for example. They need compassion, love, and the sacraments.

This woman has chosen spiritual counselors who listen. She experiences church as a supportive community quite unlike the institution she hears outsiders and former Catholics describe. She uses an analogy to illustrate her present, and happy, relationship with church.

> When my infant was ill, I did everything the doctor said to the letter. At four years old, when she's ill now I use my judgment, experience and what the doctor has to say. I question when I believe he's wrong. I feel the same about the church. I'm no longer following a lifestyle in blind obedience or fear or as some instant road to a successful life. I feel capable of considering and questioning and deciding issues for myself in the light of my faith and experience.

John Paul II continues to insist, nevertheless, that divorced Catholics who have remarried will be reconciled to the church only when they separate. If they must stay together for serious reasons, such as the children's upbringing, (certainly not for their own psychological, emotional, or sexual needs!) then they will live in complete abstinence. He reminds pastors that they must not, for whatever pretext even of a pastoral nature, perform ceremonies of any kind for divorced people who remarry, and claims that this is out of respect for the couple themselves and for the community of faithful.[15] There is a sad and serious gap here between the perception of most mid-20th century Catholics, the practice of many sensitive priests and pastors, and the voice from Rome. The Pope's position seems narrow, cold and punitive and rests on an understanding of sacrament and Christian community that is painfully out-of-step with theological reflection since Vatican Council II.

The question of divorce and remarriage in the church, like that of birth control, is one of the important items on the agenda not only for American Catholic women, but for all who would like to resolve some of the needless tension that exists now because of the widening distance between the hierarchical, Roman church and the church of the people.

Chapter Three

SEX AND IDENTITY
IN AND OUT OF
MARRIAGE:
PART TWO

Questions of Reproduction

Birth Control

THE gap between official church and the church of
the people is nowhere wider than in the question of
birth control. John Paul II has reiterated Paul VI's
pronouncement that those actions are intrinsically
evil which "either in anticipation of the conjugal act,
or in its accomplishment, or in the development of
its natural consequences, proposes, whether as an
end or as a means, to render procreation
impossible."[1] It is hardly necessary here to point out
that there is a chasm between this official teaching
and the current practice of most Catholic couples.
These couples are not selfish hedonists. They are at
least as aware as the Pope of the demands of marriage: mutual self-giving and human procreation in
the context of love. But they are infinitely closer to
the reality of married life, and subconsciously at
least recognize the inadequacy of a theology far
removed from experience.

Kathleen E. Benson, a musician serving her parish in Fairfield, Connecticut, in answer to my question "Do you agree with the church's teaching on birth control?" responded:

> No. Again back to life experience; there were years when in our marriage we were physically, mentally and emotionally spent and suffering. Four children under three years old—and they were conceived while practicing birth control the church's way. That simply doesn't work for some people and our marriage meant too much for us to continue that way when there were other options.

One woman, who had her first child owing to a faulty contraceptive device and went on happily to have six more, nevertheless finds the church's official position on birth control inconsistent, illogical and self-destructive, and finds it hard to believe it is still in force.

Because most just raise their eyebrows, shrug their shoulders and reach their own conclusions about family planning, one might think that the church's condemnation of birth control today is simply irrelevant. However, the vitality of the church's sanction was brought home to me recently when a woman in her 20's with a six-month old baby spoke of the possibility of another pregnancy in the near future. She wanted to practice some form of birth control, but her husband did not, and wondered how she could consider herself a Catholic and harbor such thoughts. Furthermore, many women, acting in ac-

cord with their consciences, are unhappy because
they feel, as one put it, "that we are in opposition to a
major teaching of our church." She continues, "I
don't feel like a hypocrite, but I think the church is
losing face and appears ambivalent."

Some look cynically upon the continued prohibition of contraception as a means of maintaining control over Catholics through the guilt evoked in them
from practicing what the church condemns.
Whatever the motivation behind the stubborn and
narrowly biological view that each and every act of
intercourse must leave open the possibility of conception, the credibility of the church as an ethical
guide suffers. Rather than accept the theological
base, which was laid during and after Vatican II, and
which would have respected a couple's moral decision concerning procreation, John Paul II has issued
a call to theologians urgently inviting them to bring
their reflections into line with the hierarchical
magisterium.[2]

There is something sadly backward about this.
Sunny Lopez, in her response to my questionnaire,
suggests that the institutional church has dem-
onstrated an appalling lack of compassion and
understanding regarding this issue. "The percentage
of women who do not comply with this church
teaching is one very strong indication that it does not
reflect the true church of believers."[3]

Since the sexual relations of couples, the transmission of life, and the nature and mission of family
embrace a range of ethical issues, and since the

church is rightly concerned about them, what sort of leadership might we welcome?

First of all, leadership which listens to the voice and experience of the people who *are* church. In this regard, it is significant that at the 1976 U.S. Bishops Conference on Liberty and Justice to All (A Call to Action) 7600 Catholics requested that the church reconsider its teaching on birth control. Only 850 Catholics supported the official position.[4]

In one sense, perhaps the most important and profound sense, the church has *already* changed its position on birth control. Until the Pope recognizes this however, many lives will be troubled and the gap between official teaching, on the one hand, and the parish priest's understanding approval as well as the practice of most Catholics, on the other hand, will be experienced as painful.

Next, in these and all other ethical questions, today's Catholics are looking for a context in which to exercise their own responsible moral judgment. In the area of sexuality, we look to those who give voice to the church's teaching to reiterate the essential value and dignity of each human being, to raise questions about the social and political implications of birth control in certain cultures, and to underscore the gravity of all that concerns the giving and nurturing of life.

The church does well to call people to question seriously their choices, and to study carefully the kinds of scientific and technological developments which affect the transmission of life. The church must also insist on the responsibility of each Christian for individual moral decisions, and must recognize the need to ask questions, such as: How will the birth of another child affect the mother's physical, psychological and emotional well-being, and that of other members of the family? What consitutes moral responsibility in matters of procreation in an overpopulated country? in economically depressed times or areas? in an age when most of the children born reach maturity?

While the majority of Catholics have resolved the matter of birth control in ways that satisfy their consciences, although labelled "immoral" by the official hierarchy, the more complex question of abortion is one which remains unresolved.

Abortion

When I asked Katie Stanley, the woman who directs Lifeline in the Robert Taylor Homes project, what ethical and moral issue she thinks the church should focus on at present, suggesting birth control, abortion, nuclear arms, and poverty among others, she had no trouble choosing: poverty is the central issue. About abortion she was ambiguous, "confused," as she put it. The question that occurs to many women is not whether it is right or wrong, she said, but, "Can I feed this child? educate this child? find room for this child?" When she looks at battered and abused children, all the arguments about the morality of abortion lose their clarity and some of their relevance. Roxane Komar of Elmhurst, Illinois, agrees, "I am divided on the issue of abortion. I'd *like* to take the no abortion stand (it's so noble), but I can't because I can imagine circumstances where abortion would be preferable. So my bottom line on this is that I believe a woman should be able to have an abortion with no questions asked or permission from anyone else needed."

In my survey of Catholic women, I posed the question "Do you think the Supreme Court decision permitting abortion should be reversed?" Of 82 respondents, 44 percent answered in the affirmative, while 30 percent thought the decision should stand. Another 20 percent described their position as ambivalent. A handful of women thought the issue should be removed completely from legal consideration, since the decision is essentially a moral one involving the woman most intimately. Mary Katherine Ryan, a lawyer practicing in Chicago, points out, however, that state legislatures made this issue a legal one by outlawing abortion. The Supreme Court decision was, therefore, necessary. She continues, "The current legal resolution can peacefully coexist with a given individual's moral decision." Some women were particularly wary of laws or amendments forbidding abortion because these would be no more effective than measures prohibiting liquor sales. One made the interesting observation that if women are forced legally to have childen what would prevent forced, legal sterilization? Four women stated their personal opposition to abortion, but were hesitant to express an opinion as to whether the Supreme Court decision should be reversed.

Joan Garvey Hermes gave an unqualified "yes" to the question. She argues:

> Abortion is sexist. It asks a women to participate in a form of schizophrenia. An unwanted child is a "bit of tissue," but a wanted child that is miscarried is to be mourned like a full-term infant. Abortion seems to me to be a largely male medical profession saying to middle class women, "We know you're incapable of handling anything difficult. Let us tidy up this mistake for you." For poor women, blacks, hispanics, abortion seems to be a form of genocide that assures fewer children on the welfare rolls. The Supreme Court decision should never have been arrived at, and should be reversed.
>
> P.S. Now let's encourage the church to take the same strong stand on war and capital punishment.

The more common argument of those emphatically and unreservedly in favor of reversing the Supreme Court decision is simply that abortion is murder. Hilda Farrell, a nurse at St. Joseph's Family Health Center in South Bend, Indiana, speaks for them in these terms, "A fertilized ovum is a child, a human being regardless of size, whether it is microscopic at the moment of conception or a seven-pound baby at birth." This position removes the moral question from *any* considertion of circumstance (the only question so removed) and from the context of women's lives.[5] Without suggesting that the taking of pre-natal life is desirable or defensible, are we to deny any consideration of the facts that sex education has been woefully inadequate, that many young women have to bear alone the full responsibility for the rearing of an unwanted child, and that the same people who condemn abortion reward certain women who refuse to have one with shame and poverty?

If women who do not share Catholic religious beliefs come, perhaps after days of panic and anguish, to the conclusion that abortion is the answer, should they have to submit to the techniques and prices of quacks who exploit them because abortion is illegal?

This is not to deny that abortion is a violent act, and that it is tragic when used as a form of birth control. But a constitutional amendment forbidding abortions would not stop them from occurring and would subject women to humiliating, costly, and unsafe methods. A Catholic woman with adult children and grandchildren, who answered my questionnaire with "a good bit of thought, consideration and introspection," makes the same point. She observes:

> The decision to have an abortion is a moral one, not legal or political. It is a personal decision involving the woman in particular, but both people involved, and should be arrived at with great consideration, counseling, and in-depth introspection. Regardless of the law, abortions have been around and will be

around as long as women get pregnant. At least, if
they are legalized, women can obtain them under
clean conditions.

Jeanne Noble, a woman with two adult, adopted
children, is another who recognizes some of the com-
plexities of the abortion issue. She finds herself on
the horns of a dilemma in answering the questions
about the desirability of reversing the Supreme Court
decision. "Lives are precious," she states, "but no
matter what the Supreme Court decides lives will be
lost, either through abortions or through improper
abortion techniques. Once again, a question of conscience and individual decision-making is involved."

None of the women who opposed the reversal of
the Supreme Court decision sees abortion on de-
mand as a good to be eagerly pursued. One remarks
that even forming an opinion about the legalization
of abortion involves painful decision. She is concerned about the effects of abortions, and wishes that
birth control would eliminate the need for them, but
she adds, "on the other hand, I have also witnessed
the battered, abused, and murdered child."

The National Assembly of Religious Women and
the National Coalition of American Nuns have given
voice to those Catholics who remain personally opposed to abortion, but nevertheless refuse to back the
movement to reverse the Supreme Court decision of
1973. NCAN's statement, released to the press in
April 1982, received considerable media coverage.
The group reiterated its opposition to abortion, then

stated its reasons for opposing the Hatch Act which would give individual states the right to legislate on the matter:

1. States vary greatly in their perception of the common good and in their enactment of laws in this regard. For example, there are some states which still do not have compulsory school attendance; others which have never formally approved voting rights for women.

2. While we continue to oppose abortion, in principle and in practice, we are likewise convinced that the responsibility for decisions in this regard resides primarily with those who are directly and personally involved.

The Coalition then called upon:

1. Decision-makers in the churches, the courts and the Congress to provide a more nurturing environment so that women will be encouraged to bring new life into the world and can be hopeful for the future of their children. It is paradoxical to us that the same leaders who are currently demanding that women bring their babies to term are simultaneously voting to cut off food stamps, child-nutrition programs, and related benefits essential for the health and well-being of our children.

2. Men everywhere, to educate themselves and one another on the responsibilities of fatherhood. Intercourse must be seen by men as only the beginning of a solemn and holy relationship, and fatherhood as a role which requires continuing nurturance and

material assistance to the mother and the child.
3. Women everywhere, to disavow the use of abortion as a normative means of birth control and to
educate themselves in ways of being creatively
responsible—insofar as this is possible—for avoiding
unwanted pregnancies.

Of the 600 letters received by NCAN, 66 percent
supported their position. Many of the letters are sad,
human documents which chronicle the sexual abuse
of women through rape and incest. Victims of
violence, they then became bearers of false guilt.
NCAN's statement gave them hope.

David O'Brien Connelly of the *Shreveport Journal*
(Louisiana), in his letter to NCAN, called the statement "...a model of Christian principle—one
inspired and informed by the Holy Spirit." He
continues:

It is the most humane statement I have seen issued
by a group of religious in the Catholic church...You
remain opposed to abortion, but ever ready to support women, in Christian love, who decide on one.

Those of us opposed to abortion can spend our
energies in better ways than in backing an amendment which threatens any woman considering an
abortion with legal punishment. We can work for a
society in which women are supported emotionally
and financially in their pregnancies, in which low-
cost childcare benefits are available to them, in

which men bear equal responsibility with women faced with an unexpected pregnancy, and in which so-called illegitimate children are welcomed and nourished. We can, as Catholic women, encourage church and state to support research into safe and adequate means of birth control, means which would encourage men as well as women to assume responsibility in this area. We can further the education of teen-agers in responsible sexual behavior. We can look beyond abortion and join in the search for the kind of personal, social, and technological discoveries which will eventually make abortion a non-problem. Meanwhile, we can reiterate the moral obligation of women to insist on their personal responsibility (not exercised in a vacuum, however) in matters concerning childbearing. Bishops and statesmen can neither relieve them of that responsibility nor deprive them of that privilege.

Being Single

Books about singles have a distinctly different ring nowadays. In 1969, Rebecca Greer in a book entitled *Why Isn't a Nice Girl Like You Married?* claimed to give advice which would enable a single "girl" to live happily on her own—anywhere. But some of the burning questions she set out to answer were: How do you play the mating game—and win? How do you meet—and keep—the men you want? What are the real facts about late marriage? Can you really make yourself more attractive? She clearly sees the single state as pre-marital (if everything goes right). But in a recently published book, *Our Lives for Ourselves*,[6] Nancy Peterson sets out to see who the single woman is, the quality of her life at various "passages," the single's contentment and problems. She sees the single woman as one who reflects the human situation, as one who has the same human needs, faces the same challenges to become whole, and experiences similar kinds of conflicts and resolutions as everyone else. She manages to do what Mary Jo Weaver called for in an article a few years ago, namely, pose questions about the single state in terms of wholeness, that is, not simply in terms of relations (who the single is or isn't living with), but in terms of who singles *are*.[7]

I will be concerned here mainly with the never-married, or in the less negative term sometimes employed by Peterson, the ever-single. Among women, this group constitutes a small five to seven percent.

While it is clear that the vast majority of women choose to conform to the social norm, and to meet their need for love, intimacy, security, service, and companionship within the family structure, the choice of some women to meet these needs elsewhere should come as less of a shock in an age when psychologists, sociologists, and married women themselves have revealed the deleterious effects upon women of the institution of marriage. The family may be the cornerstone of the social structure, but traditionally the institution has furthered the interests of fathers and sons and too often propped a social structure in which women were to know their proper and subordinate place. The push is on for more egalitarian marriages, and some couples are actually attaining them, but women see the advantages of them more clearly than men and the latter may be slow to surrender the comforts and services associated with having a wife. Married women are often economically dependent, and some research suggests that they enjoy less robust psychological and physical health than the never-married. Furthermore, divorce, a more and more common phenomenon, frequently affects the woman more adversely than the man. If she is over thirty and has children, she is less likely to remarry than the man, should she want to, and less likely to be able to command the salary she needs to support herself and children. Whatever the rewards of marriage for women, the fact that some women choose to remain on their own should not really be cause for mystification. Nor should these women be pitied or patronized. Neither should we assume them to be selfish simply because they value their freedom and their personal autonomy.

Perhaps we need a theology of being single. Theologians have struggled with a theology of marriage, and have struggled to update it; and they have developed a theology of the religious life, but being a vowed celibate is a very particular way of being single. Nancy Hardesty in an article in the *Daughters of Sarah*[8] suggests a taking off point for a theology of being single: for Christians, singleness should be the reference point, rather than marriage. She quotes a Mennonite theologian, John Howard Yoder, who reminds us that singleness is the first normal state for all of us, and that while existing marriages should be nurtured, there exists no Christian imperative to become married as soon as we can or to prefer marriage over singleness as more whole or wholesome.

On the other hand, why must there be reference points which categorize us in terms of whether or not we have, or have ever had, a marriage partner? In my own questionnaire I devised questions for the single, married, divorced, widowed, and members of religious orders, and then reflected that I had fallen into the trap of defining women once more in terms of their "marital status." Relationships, of course, are important in our self-definition, but as Hardesty points out, Jesus' paradigm for his own relationships was not marriage but friendship. Indeed, even in marriage, the spouse as friend may be the deepest and most satisfying element of the relationship.

Human needs are the same for all: satisfying personal relationships, intimacy, work that is recognized, personal autonomy in adulthood, reasonable access to health, leisure and economic self-sufficiency. In a Christian community these should be the goals of married and single alike, and each should help all attain them.

Parish activity, however, is often family-centered. One single woman observes, "Everything but the CCN fashion show tickets are for couples. Families are the primary emphasis and the family emphasis is on a 1950's level. There is little done to promote the family's awareness of the outside world"—eloquent testimony to the fact that too many parishes fail to take into account the growing numbers of never-married, separated, divorced, or widowed. One of the divorced women who responded to my questionnaire, for instance, observes:

> I am an annulled, "practicing" Catholic—a rarity among my fellow career women and even among my SWORD (Separated, Widowed, or Divorced Catholics) parish group who get reinforcement from their separated and divorced peers, but interestingly not from the liturgy or parish main-stream. SWORD seems to be their lifeline to the Church, assuring them they haven't been kicked out! This saddens me a great deal.

And the professional women, mostly single, in a small discussion and support group in Mount Carmel Parish in Chicago, point out that they find in one another and in the parish what they were not able to find in their own home parishes: generally good sermons, a congregation that is mixed ethnically and economically, a sense of community, and the opportunity to reflect on what it means to be a woman in today's church. One of them, Maureen Donlan, 22, said her age group is neglected in most parishes, especially if one is single. The women's group is a way for her to overcome a feeling of alienation and of becoming more spiritually active.

The women noted that their sense of alienation in the church sprang essentially from the resistance of the church to women's ministry, and the discomfort of the clergy with single women. Rita Carmody said her attendance at the Sunday liturgy at St. Clement's became a much more fruitful experience after the addition of Dolores Brooks, O.P. to the pastoral team. This single fact renewed her experience of church. It has mitigated her feeling that "at times that the church views me as a non-person. I have also felt at times that my interests were not best served by a celibate, male clergy who were more suspicious and guarded with women than compassionate and understanding." The other women agreed that many priests are unable to deal with single women as persons. Their seminary training feeds suspicion of women, and they perceive the sexual activity of single women as especially suspect. The sexuality of religious women and married women, after all, is controlled. Who knows what single women are up to?

These women find in the discussion group a kind of base community where they can re-center and energize one another. Elayne Hill has experienced a renewed sense of hope and of self-confidence through the listening and search of the group. Still, the women have no formal tie with the parish since the departure of Sr. Mary Jane Griffin, the associate pastor who brought the group together. They are on the margin of parish life.

These women, and others like them, are not

especially looking for activities for singles. They are looking for spiritual and intellectual renewal, for a common reflection on scripture, for education on social issues, for an awareness of women as working, thinking beings. They have much to offer a parish. Those who organize parish activities would do well to consider the question that Mary Jo Weaver asks in the article cited: "How can single people function to mitigate against some of the problems in society, especially problems in the family and in churches, and get their own needs met at the same time?" The challenge is to bring people together not on the basis of their "state in life," but on the basis of their common human search for love, support, encouragement, and opportunities to think, give, and grow. The separtion of groups into the divorced, widowed, and separated, other singles, and married couples may have some justification, but people in each of those categories would have much to gain by forging closer ties. The suspicions and taboos that now keep them apart deserve reexamination in the light of the Gospel. Those responsible for any aspect of parish life must take seriously the charge of the single woman who wrote, "I don't think the church knows what to do with us and would rather not think about us if possible."

Another questionnaire respondent agrees:

> We are looked upon as a nothing—our lifestyle or needs are simply ignored. We are acknowledged *maybe*, if we take care of our parents or somebody

else's children. The clergy have nothing to offer our
needs, or have little understanding of how they can
help singles develop a healthy life-style or self-image.

This woman found no help in the church in her
discovery that one can be "great and good and still
be single." Ann Clark, on the other hand, finds that
church and clergy do offer moral and emotional support, but little intellectual stimulation.

Few of the single women referred to sexual needs
or sexual relationships. One did volunteer that she
has not fully complied with church teaching about
pre-marital sex or birth control. Another, in answer
to the question "How would you characterize the attitude of the clergy toward single women" replied:
"This varies greatly. Some treat women as children
and are patronizing. Others as sex-objects (I have
been accosted by five different priests). Others, for-
tunately, treat women as intellectual equals." The
perils and needs of singles in the matter of sexual
behavior will vary enormously, but it is clear that a
sexual ethic which quite simply, totally and forever
deprives singles of sexual expression is inadequate.
Single women in the church need support as they
search for ways to satisfy their need for intimacy.
They need encouragement to risk, because this is an
essential aspect of self-discovery and growth. In a
church whose people stress sexual responsibility and
minimize sexual regulation, single women will know
at each stage of their lives how to avoid being sexually repressed on the one hand, or sexually exploited

on the other. They will know, above all, how to value themselves and their achievements whether they choose celibacy or choose a commitment involving sexual expression, whether they remain single or eventually marry; and in either state they will continually strive for that balance of autonomy and interdependence which marks healthy adulthood.

Vowed Celibacy

A new theology of sexuality has at once rescued the married from a state of being second-class Christians, and raised questions about the meaning of lifelong virginity "for the kingdom." Most reasonable people are ready to admit that each state has its advantages and its hazards, its possibilities for growth and its restrictions; that neither represents a superior form of witness to Christ *per se* and that individuals in both ways of life are called to holiness and to love as Christ loved. "Marriage and virginity or celibacy are two ways of expressing and living the one mystery of the covenant of God with his people," writes John Paul II.[9] One regrets that further on he reverts to claiming superiority for celibacy "by reason of the singular link which it has with the kingdom of God." The religious does not have to be assured that celibacy is superior in order to be convinced that it has meaning. For her it is one valid way of giving witness to a personal commitment to Christ and to unreserved service to the Christian community and to the world.

If those who marry are freer now to integrate the sexual expression of their love into their quest for holiness, religious are more and more conscious that their commitment to the kingdom and their vow of celibacy does not preclude human love and friendship with both sexes. The call to holiness and to meaningful service, indeed, requires a deep capacity for these things, as does the healthy development of the personality of the celibate.

Women religious are more willing today to face and discuss honestly their need for intimacy and for expression of the sexual dimension of their personhood in the context of their vow. Elizabeth Kriener, O.P., confides, "The church's teaching about sexuality contributed to my fear of risking intimacy on even the intellectual, psychological or spiritual level," but today she and countless others are being freed from negative attitudes through visionary persons like Evelyn and Jim Whitehead, and through honest explorations of the meaning of sexuality and the celibate choice such as Donald Goergen, O.P. pursues in his book *The Sexual Celibate*.[10]

New insights gained from workshops, reading and personal experience must be backed by support from a community which believes in the value of deep friendships within and outside of the community. In an atmosphere of love and trust, the religious will be able to work out the tensions involved in reconciling the demands of community with those of friendship; the need for intimacy with fidelity to her vow.

The contribution of women religious will be important in the continuing search to articulate the meaning and value of celibacy. It will help redefine celibacy at many levels: those of personal experience, community witness, and religious symbol. The question will continue to be relevant whether or not marriage becomes an option for the diocesan priest, because celibacy in religious orders is not accidental, but integral, to the life choice.

Homosexuality

I am a lesbian. It is an understatement to say that Church teaching on homosexuality is painful. What is even more painful is that that teaching is based on a male understanding of sexuality (however misinformed) and, again, renders lesbianism invisible. I find references to "female homosexuals" token at best. The misogyny of this teaching seems impenetrable.

The same young woman who wrote the above was also able to say that while her experience as a Catholic lesbian has been painful, the church has also been a source of love and healing, mainly through contact, both professional and social, with women religious and through her professional work in diocesan social action offices. She adds:

Survival dictates that I surround myself with like-minded women (let me tell you, Christian lesbian feminists are hard to find) even more than with gay

men who are, sadly, as sexist as their hetero counterparts. It is lonely to be in this position—yet I manage
to get what I need.

Her choice to remain active in the church has been
challenged by her lesbian friends. The challenge of
answering their questions, she says, has helped her
to distinguish between the essence of her faith and
its patriarchal trappings. This young woman may be
a rarity in the church. The fact that she exists at all is
hopeful. She is finding within some church structures intellectual stimulation, and moral support.
She is co-chair of an organization working for
pastoral ministry to lesbian and gay Catholics, but
like other well-adjusted homosexuals she is not fix-
ated on the question of sexual orientation, whether
her own or others'. Like any psychologically healthy
person, she is sure of her self-worth and dignity, confident of her lovability and of her power to love, and
engaged in satisfying work dealing with a variety of
social justice issues.

This young woman's personal journey from believing she was flawed to genuine self-acceptance corresponds to a similar movement in the church and
society at large. Homosexuality, once viewed as a
defect, a depravity, and a contagious disease, is increasingly accepted as a psychosexual orientation
which can serve as the basis for a constructive
expression of human love. At the very least, most
people concede that lesbians and gays should not be
persecuted or denied their civil rights.

The official church position is that while a
his or her sexual
of that preference,
...n or gay who acts
immorally. In this
...ld consist, in part,
...lves to a life of
...ns, however, have
is the "norm" and
...nnot attain it, nor
to remain celibate;
...ationships, striving
genital sexual rela-
Charles Curran put
...ational Symposium
...lic Church held in
1981. This goes a
...wo evils" argument
...sexual relationships
...romiscuity, but are
...sordered. John J.
enjoys the *imprimi*
...es the church to go
...al and moral reflec-
...sitive approach in
the notion that all

*My Whole Being Proclaims
The Greatness Of The Lord.*

Luke 1:46

*Souvenir of my 50th
Anniversary of Profession
1934 - 1984*

*Give Thanks To God
With Me.*

*Sister Therese of the Infant Jesus, OCD
Carmel of Elysburg*

moral theology would p...

individuals are heterosexual unless something goes wrong (faulty family relations; weak hormones; perverse forms of seduction), and start from the vantage point that homosexuality may be part of the divine plan and play an intrinsic role in human society. He urges moral theologians to undertake the difficult task of determining the *why* of homosexuality, not in the sense of an abnormality that must be explained, but in the sense of its final purpose.

> For on its discovery depends both the ability of the homosexual to accept himself or herself with true self-love and understanding and the ability of the heterosexual society to accept a homosexual minority, not just as objects of pity and tolerance at best, but as their equals capable of collaborating in the mutual task of building a more humane society.[12]

What role might homosexuality play in the general economy of human relations? It might, together with the women's movement, successfully challenge the damaging sex-stereotypes which render both men and women half-persons. Homosexuals might be able to model love between equals as a surer foundation for married couples than the assumptions that now dictate the role-playing of many. They might, as Richard Woods proposes in his book on homosexuality and spirituality, demonstrate that "male-female relationships can exist on the basis of mere personal attraction, by choice in friendship (*philia*) rather than *eros*. Such a realization is not only beautiful and valuable in itself, it is also liberating, for it frees us from our fears of same-sex friendships...."[13]

Neither of these authors attempts to hide the negative, compulsive, or destructive elements that may be associated with the world of homosexuals, but they invite us to consider the part that fear, ignorance and persecution from straight society has played in posing some of the moral struggles faced by lesbians and gays. A self-accepting homosexual community, sure of its own dignity and of respect from all sectors of society, would be one less liable to bend to what Woods refers to as the "sinful social forces of the gay world."

While lesbianism is mentioned briefly here and there in these books, they, like most Catholic studies of homosexuality focus on male homosexuality. For an idea of the force and meaning of lesbianism, one can turn to Mary Daly. She points out that the dichotomy set up between hetero-and homosexuality has its origin in patriarchalism, a system in which men stand to benefit by the power and status which sex-role stereotyping confers upon them.[14] Male fear and hostility toward homosexuals is based on the anxiety that this power will be lost if men refuse to play their assigned role. Feminists, in rejecting patriarchal categories, render the terms homosexual and heterosexual irrelevant, and re-define homosexual as a deep and intimate relationship with a person of the same sex, with or without genital activity. Judgments about either homosexual or heterosexual relationships are based not on the biological identity of the persons involved, but on the quality of the relationship. Daly in this book warned against the setting up of new dogmas concerning sexual behavior, and left room for the choice of men as sex partners even for those who challenged the injustices of a sexist society.

In *Gyn/Ecology* the accent is different, and Mary Daly moves with the radical left to the position that women who are psychosexually bound to men (whose social conditioning renders them destructive in relationship to women) cannot be free to explore the world beyond patriarchy. In this world women together move in our own time/space enspiriting and sparking one another, dis-covering the integrity of women's be-ing.[15]

Mary Daly, whose roots are in Catholicism, has moved out not only of that tradition but even of Christianity. Every woman, however, stands to gain in the presence of this original and forceful thinker in the women's movement. She obliges each of us to examine our lives, our relationships, and our possibilities while inviting us to have the courage to *see*.

A feminist within the church, Mary E. Hunt, sees the development of a new theology of sexuality as the particular challenge of the North American church and a condition of its entrance into the 21st century as a liberation community.[16] Coming to terms with sexuality and with the issues of birth control, abortion, divorce and remarriage, premarital sex, priestly celibacy, and homosexuality will mark the church's passage to adulthood, says Hunt. Dealing with them, we will come to terms at the same time with questions of authority: who decides what is right and good under particular circumstances, who exerts moral influence, who is church? The answer does not, of course, lie in blanket approval of all of the above, but the church risks entering the next century "divided, damaged, and neurotic" if the gap between responsible decisions made by individuals in good faith and official, universal prohibition is not closed. We need not worry, as does the narrator of *Father's Day*, that the poetry of the old church will go with its discipline. "How can you think human beings are tragically noble if you've no way to feel guilty about anything?" he asked.[17] There will be plenty of tragic nobility, plenty of guilt, but now over the right things.

Perhaps women in the church have a particular mission in this regard. It is certain that a sexual ethic, and indeed, a truly human ethic in general, cannot be formulated without us. Nor can the work of the church be carried on effectively without our full and equal participation in it—which brings us to the question of women and ministry.

Chapter Four

WOMEN AND THE CHURCH'S MISSION

Ministry in Today's Church

IN the years since Vatican II, Catholics have slowly but steadily been revising their notion of the nature and mission of the church and the responsibility of church members in that mission. The revision is far from complete, and insight, expectation, and practice may vary greatly from diocese to diocese, parish to parish, and parishioner to parishioner. But gradually, owing to the exchange of knowledge, vision, and experience between scholars and ministers, laity, religious and clergy, and among churches, increasing numbers of Catholics appreciate today the implications of a move from church as power structure to church as community. The refinement of historical method over the last century, and the consequent deepening and broadening of historical consciousness and imagination, have enabled us to put this and other recent changes into perspective. We can see them now not as dangerous departures from divine ordinances, but simply as the most recent in a series of attempts to keep God's word alive in changing circumstances.

The church of the 80's sees itself not as removed

from the world, inimical and superior to it, but as part of a world called to participate in Christ's own mission "to bring the good news to the poor, to proclaim liberty to captives and to the blind new sight, to set the downtrodden free..." (Luke, 4:18-19). The message will take on different accents in different times and places, and will be carried out in different forms of ministry as societal patterns shift and needs change, but central to it will be a search for meaning, for values beyond the tangible, for the ability to recognize the sacred in the unfolding of every life and of every aspect of the universe.

It is becoming increasingly clear to us that the message is communicated most effectively when it is spoken through the lives of "ordinary" Christians. If, in the recent past, Catholics tended to identify church with hierarchy and to wait for the truth to be preached from the pulpit, if we were likely to conceive of ministering as something that priests and religious did to the laity, we have since Vatican II moved toward a concept of church and ministry much closer to the understanding of the church in New Testament times. We have moved away, that is, from a view of church as a tightly organized, highly structured pyramid with leadership and authority vested heavily at the top, a church in which ministers enjoy a kind of caste privilege, and authority is exercised and expressed in exhaustive, legal detail. This characterization does not, of course, adequately describe the fullness of church life from the Constantinian period till mid-twentieth century. But we recognize the general contours. And the contours are not those of community.

In what Schillebeeckx distinguishes as the fourth phase in the evolution of leadership roles in the church[1] we are beginning to soften the rigid lines of the pyramid to a form more closely resembling a circle, a form that better accommodates a community. We recognize the historical conditions that gave rise to the hierarchized structure that gradually emerged as the church order, and painfully conscious of its limitations, struggle toward forms which at once better suit our own times and more closely resemble apostolic times.

In this fourth phase, each member of the community is called upon to witness, to minister, to proclaim the word, to exercise the universal priesthood of believers, to make forgiveness visible, to be a sign of unity and hope. The combined activity of its individual members in worship, study, teaching, preaching, and mutual service is precisely what constitutes church. And the lines between official and non-official ministry become blurred and less important as each member, according to individual gifts, joins in the effort to witness to the community's faith, to be present to the needs of one another in the local community, and to play some part in the global struggles that mark our times.

This summary of a growing consensus in regard to the nature of the church and to the mutual obligations of its members to build a Christian community which can serve as a model of sanity, justice, and

love to a divided world must not be confused, of
course, with the often disheartening reality of life in
the local parish where ordained priesthood may still
be the standard for preaching, ministry, and con-
sultation on parish affairs, and is certainly the condition for presiding at the liturgy. But the movement
toward de-clericalization of the church is on. It
gained impetus at Vatican II, where voices from the
past as well as voices of the future spoke. The voices
of the future have gained strength in the intervening
years, and Catholics are more and more looking
upon the compromises of Vatican II as the marks of
an age of transition. Many are impatient for the
dawn of a new age, and none more so, perhaps, than
women.

Women and Ministry

> After years of forming a conscience that is sensitive
> to the needs of others and wanting to put that sen-
> sitivity and ability to good use, I am restricted from
> front line service, e.g. the diaconate program or high
> level decision-making...I think the church better
> find a way for women to more fully share and par-
> ticipate in life-giving, faith-filled service (other than
> having large families.)

So writes Bonnie Williams, an articulate suburban
mother of four. Her husband is in the diaconate program. Because she is a woman, her role in that program is one of supporter and on-looker. Her words
remind us that the "new" ecclesiology has gaping

holes, and that the appealing vision of church as
community, and of the laity assuming a full share in
the ministry and leadership of the church, will not
and cannot be realized until women's gifts are
recognized and women are, throughout the church,
accepted at every level of ministry for which they are
qualified. "To say that there are some Christian
ministries that are limited by sex is to say that no one
is obliged to the whole gospel. Some demands of the
gospel are male; some female."[2]

The exclusion of women from the diaconate and
from priesthood has not prevented women from participating in a wider range of ministries than ever
before in the history of the church. Women earn
higher degrees in every field of religious studies;
they carry on the work of evangelization in mission
territories where they outnumber men two to one;
they are parish administrators, teachers at every
level of instruction, catechists, directors of Scripture
study groups, vicars of religious, pastoral associates,
retreat directors, counsellors, staff members in peace
and justice centers, and hospital and college
chaplains. They bring professional skills together
with ministerial concern to a wide range of activities
in the fields of medicine and social services. Is there,
then, no problem? The problem is that women are
not given equal access to these positions; when they
do attain them they are often not given sufficient
support; they are frequently underpaid or expected
to volunteer their time and services, and often their
co-workers are slow to give up stereotypic and sexist
assumptions.

A few quotations from questionnaire respondents will underscore the point.

> I work for the church. I feel frustrated by church attitudes of hierarchy and office and defensiveness. I find the pay scale insulting. I find the internal church is a contradiction—a countersign to the message of Jesus.

> Women should be given equal opportunities for full participation in the church's ministry. The same resources available to men should be available to women, i.e. financial resources, scholarship funds. Education, consciousness-raising and structural change should occur from the parish level up. We could start with church language.

Barbara Perry of Mount Vernon, Ohio points out that women's experience differs, depending on the age and education of the pastor. Having worked in and for the church for 27 years, she now finds herself with the title of Coordinator of Religious Education, but feels that "office clerk" would be more descriptive, since she has no control over the budget, and is generally asked to do detailed office work rather than to generate ideas or make policy decisions. The situation would improve, she suggests, if seminary faculties would include married couples and non-religious singles. Present faculties only reinforce biased, sexist attitudes. Finally, celibacy should be made optional. Barbara Perry concludes with a statement that gives eloquent expression to current disillusionment with clericalism, on the one hand,

and on the other to the universal call to build the church: "I used to pray that one of my six sons would be a priest. Now I pray that God will use them to make the church grow in Jesus and in Spirit. This is a religious vocation."

Catholic universities have not been any more enlightened than many parishes in regard to the women in their midst. Discriminatory practices in hiring, promotion and salary are blatant, but because the double standard is pervasive officials are apparently blind to them. Federal probes at Marquette and Fordham, and suits filed by women at Canisius College (Buffalo, N.Y.) and Notre Dame in the last two years are helping to open eyes in the arena of the Church's ministry in higher education.

Underlying the insistent call for real equality between men and women in the church, a call that is equally strong among women religious and lay women, is the realization that this will entail basic structural and attitudinal changes. Few of the women who answered my questionnaire characterized themselves as feminists, but it was clear that they shared Mary E. Hunt's conviction that the "add women and stir" approach to Roman Catholic ministry was not the answer.[3]

The introduction of women into present orders and models of leadership, into the "brotherhood," is not the point. A recurrent theme among women who gather to speak, reflect, or theologize about church is that the distinction made between the sexes is prototypic of other distinctions made in church and society between the more and less powerful, and the

powerless. In the same breath that women speak
about the need of including women at each stage of
church development, mission and future planning,
they speak of the need to erode power structures
which contradict the gospel, and the need to disman-
tle the barriers between rich and poor, black and
white, clergy and laity, women religious and lay
women. One questionnaire respondent put it simply,
"The church could become a model for all of society
by changing the structure and showing how people
can really be respected for who they are—no power
structure."

Women and Priesthood

Does the elimination of traditional modes of
church structure and authority imply the elimination
of ordained priesthood? Are those women misguided
who seek women's ordination, since by doing so they
risk reinforcing a clericalist view of the church and
perpetuating the oppressive structures under which
women have suffered? I have outlined my views on
this question in the chapter on "Women" in *Tomorrow's Church*[4], and return to the question only briefly
here. I do so partly because the question was raised
repeatedly by the women who answered the questionnaire, usually in answer to the question: "Has
equality been realized in church structures and practice?" Typical answers were:

Are women serving as priests? Do they preach the
word?

Practice is a more valid indicator of belief than stated policy. There are no women priests—that says it all.

Kathleen Miller, a young married professional, answered the question negatively, but went on:

I'm not convinced it matters much. For all the men might think, church structure is one of the least significant aspects of the church. Even Jesus wasn't impressed by it (nor it by Him). God hasn't enforced boundaries on gifts and ministries.

For some, then, ordination is a sort of litmus test for equality, for others it is irrelevant for the mutual service which Christians render one another and the world according to their gifts. The two sets of responses reflect differing emphasis on office and charism. As Alcuin Coyle points out, women have always played an important charismatic role in the church, but are now seeking a more permanent place (office) in institutions. But they are doing so, he continues, from a strong, prophetic stance.[5]

The fact is there must be some institutionalization of ministries if the Christian community is to maintain its identity, but those called to leadership in office must beware of sclerosis and remain open to the possibilities of new socio-cultural situations. A revitalization of church institutions in today's world depends on women's full incorporation into them. Women are especially attuned to what Schillebeeckx has termed "...the necessary unity in tension between charisma and its institutionalization."[6]

Less seduced by power than most men, but aware of the advantages of official recognition, women are keenly aware that "Ministry without charisma becomes starved and threatens to turn into a power institution; charisma without any institutionalization threatens to be volatilized into fanaticism and pure subjectivity...."[7] Women in the church are not asking for entrance into a privileged rank; neither are they content to carry on the church's work while an all-male contingent maintains final control of decisions and policy, shapes the church's ethics, and preaches and presides at eucharists.

As present structures weaken, as less and less credence is given to present models of priesthood, and as fewer and fewer men present themselves for ordination, women will play and, indeed, are already playing an indispensable role in creating new forms of leadership in the church. "Ordination" may, in the church that is slowly fashioning itself, mean recognition on the part of a community of its spontaneous leaders, male and female, and of the particular gifts which enable them to embody Christ's love, to keep alive his Spirit, to preach his Word, to heal, reconcile, and give witness to unity. These members will preside at the eucharist which gives expression to all of this.

If the new church is to be born, women must be willing to engage in experiments. Schillebeeckx demonstrates the necessity for experiment in a living church, and especially in times when a given church

order, because of shifts in social and cultural patterns, begins to obstruct what it was meant to ensure,
namely the building up of a Christian community.[8]
Experiments at the grass-roots level, by stimulating
consciousness and making new forms visible,
prepare the way for official and approved changes.
This is part of the church's history; this is in line
with the church's teaching. Christians are to obey the
will of God as mediated through the church, but also
as manifested in the "signs of the times." When these
conflict, a person whose conscience has been tested
must act in accord with that conscience and with the
needs of the Christian community. It is in this context that women have gathered and broken bread.
And women must continue to do so, not just among
themselves, but in mixed communities. And they
must continue to preach and to object to the
downgrading of their preaching by having it
relegated outside the eucharistic celebration or having it termed "reflection" instead of homily. When it
becomes clear that the sky does not fall in, that God's
gifts of leadership are not dispensed on the basis of
sex, and that it is an enriching experience for all concerned when women and men drop their roles and
interact as equals, then it will become possible for
new practices to move from the margin to the center
of church life and to enjoy official approbation.

Blacks would still be riding in the back of the bus
in the South if they had not had the courage to step
"illegally" across the barrier. When tradition has
sanctioned discriminatory practices, and when these

have become institutionalized in law, at first it takes powerful skills of persuasion and organization to effect the slightest change. It also takes a willingness to accept unflattering labels and to be the object of threats, and various forms of ostracism. But as consciousness is transformed, what seemed at first unthinkable becomes possible and then normal and finally desirable. The American church is ready for this progression in what concerns the ecclesial role of women and their exercise of every form of ministry.

Women's Experience/Women's View

In emphasizing what women bring to ministry, we run the risk of falling into the old trap of stereotypes, and of exacerbating divisions and dualisms which operate, ultimately, to keep men in positions of authority and women in satellite and secondary positions. Tracts which assume that there are clearly distinct masculine and feminine natures, and that the role of women in the church will be determined by an examination of the nature of their specific charism precisely as women must be suspect. Such is the well-meaning text of the Pastoral Commission of the Sacred Congregation for the Evangelization of Peoples entitled "The Role of Women in Evangelization."[9] The piece contains valuable insights, and calls for greater responsibility and independence for women in ministry. It makes the point specifically that the extent of women's ministry should not be

determined by the availability or shortage of priests
or male personnel, but by what women wish to do
and can do. But there are strange hesitations.
"Feminine qualities" will be useful in administrative
tasks and in pastoral ones, but women's pastoral
activities will not constitute ministries "in the strict
sense." Why not? Women will, in certain cases, administer baptism and preside at marriages, but the
role of women at other functions, such as the prayers
for the sick and at funerals, should be the object
of further study. Why? The commission assures
bishops and clergy that women's requests to be
entrusted with greater pastoral responsibilities
spring from their distress at the sight of neglected
Christian communites and not from "a spirit of
pretension." Why is this assurance necessary when
women offer their services? Are seminarians tested
for a spirit of pretension, a tendency toward ar-
rogance, a touch of elitism? The authors hope that
"to the consecrated women's offer of their service,
the authorities will reply with sympathetic action, to
the full range of possibilities, which are many." Why
just consecrated women? And why should women
have to depend on the luck of the draw which deter-
mines whether their local pastor or bishop will look
kindly on their request to exercise the ministries for
which they are qualified? Women are frustrated
precisely because certain clerics and bishops are incapable of dealing with women as equals and co-
workers. Women are willing to be subject to the same
criteria as men in the exercise of their ministry, but if

the possession of lauded "feminine" qualities and special charisms, so valuable in the church's work, keeps them in a perpetual state of humble suppliant, it may be tempting to shed them.

Whatever the limitations of this document, its authors are on to something. For if we must avoid reverting to stereotypes, it would be foolish to deny that women's conditioning and experience have been different from men's. The differences we observe are not universal, nor are they attributable to nature. And we must be wary of reading them in such a way as to reinforce political, social, and economic inequities. If women are, indeed, deft, methodical, and have an eye for detail, for instance, why not encourage them to become brain surgeons rather than low-paid fabricators of computer chips? And in an age when the present power structure of the church frustrates its own aims, why not use women's creativity, women's concept of what leadership means and how it is to be used, not only in positions such as Directors of Religious Education, but at the helm of parishes and dioceses?

This is as hard for women to envisage as it is for bishops to imagine a woman in their midst. And most women feel, not so much incapable of the tasks involved, as repelled by the notion of entering the ranks of the "princesses of the church," wielding authority over all "below." But women's service in leadership can be part of the evolution of new patterns of governance. In a book of fascinating insight into the meaning and workings of power and the political process, Elizabeth Janeway remarks:

> ...when the weak habitually turn their backs on
> power because they accept the stereotypes that
> undervalue them, they permit their rulers to define
> proper processes of governing according to the
> experience of the rulers alone, so that it comes to
> seem that only one "right way" to handle power ex-
> ists.[10]

Women's superiority in the area of personal relations, their intuition, their sensitivity, their respect
for the slow development of persons, their ability to
judge character, to listen, to nourish, to build community, their capacity for adaptation, their
preference for collegial forms of governing: none of
this, surely, constitutes an impediment to leadership.
These are the very qualities that are needed to show
that there are many ways to handle power in the
church. They are the human qualities that will help
ensure that the church is a place where life can
flourish. The sooner they become characteristics of
all who minister and lead in the church, the better off
we all will be.

The "powers of the weak" are particularly useful
in times of change and transition, in stressful times.
In calm and settled times where the *status quo* reigns
unquestioned, the talents of the powerless are under-
utilized, and, in fact, barely recognized except as
they serve the needs of the powerful. When the
established order outlives its relevance, however,

and begins to crack, then the creativity of the governed finds new scope, and the values ordinarily assigned to the weak (women, the poor, minorities) are thrown into relief. These include a concern for community and cooperation rather than a desire to conquer, master and control. No one will dispute the fact that these are times of change for church and society, times that require fresh vision, and the dynamism that can result from the confrontation and gradual meshing of the different world of men and women, rich and poor, black and white. These "signs of the times" must be read closely by all who are concerned for the church's future.

Collaboration

Promise and Problems

Men's and women's work in the church, as in the home and in the business world, has been until recently separate and well-defined. In the parish, sisters ran the school, priests exercised the sacramental and pastoral ministry, lay people, men and women, met in associations which organized various social events and raised money for the parish. Today, when a sister may be a pastoral associate, a lay woman principal of the parish school, and when the parish staff brings together men and women, ordained and unordained, there is promise for renewed ministry; there is also inevitable tension. Differing expectations, changing behavior and power patterns, and the crumbling of once-secure roles which helped established identity, complicate staff or team relationships.

There are abundant potential sources of friction among ordained, religious, and laity without introducing the dimension of gender, but gender differences are often basic to the misunderstanding and frustration which can hinder the work of the team. Anne Wilson Schaef, a psychotherapist, sketches the widely different approaches of the dominant White Male System and of the emerging Female System to crucial elements of our life and culture: time, relationships, power, love, sexuality, friendship, leadership, rules, decision-making, communication, commitment, responsibility, and morality.[11] To point up a few: men are more likely to want to control, women to understand differences and "process" them; men look upon leading as being out front and presenting an all-knowing and powerful image, women see leadership as an opportunity to facilitate and to bring out from each the best she has to offer a project; in the male system, rules may take precedence over individuals, in the female system they are more likely to serve the needs of the individual; men in negotiation are out to win and often do so through manipulation or bluff, women enter into negotiation with the goal of reaching a mutual agreement in which as many needs as possible are met for both parties; men look upon honesty in communication as a dangerous letting down of defenses, women look upon it as a necessary basis for understanding and being understood; for men responsibility involves an accountability-blame system, for women it means the ability to respond to needs; men reach decisions through Robert's Rules and rejoice if their side wins even by the slimmest of majorities; women are capable of following the rules, but prefer to reach decisions through consensus; men look upon friends as buddies, women expect in friendship a mutual revelation of self; men look upon power as something to hoard, women as something to share; women know the way the man's world operates since they must in order to survive in it; men are unaware that systems other than their own exist. Is it any wonder that collabortive efforts have floundered and sometimes failed?

Much of the difficulty in establishing good working relationships on teams including women and men can be explained by the fact that their training, experience, and view of relationships differ considerably. Schaef points out that men tend to behave as if the persons involved in a relationship must be either one-up or one-down. Women who have come to know and trust their own system, generally consider relationships to be peer unless proven otherwise.[12] The assumption of equality is an important element in true collaboration. It is one that women working together do not have to struggle to establish. This is true, of course, among women religious who have come to a new and deeper understanding of relationships in community since Vatican II.

A Female Model

If I single out the collaborative experience of women religious as a female model, I do not mean to suggest that there is something *innately* feminine in it, or that it is unique to religious communities. I choose it because it is the model of collaboration I am most familiar with and because I believe it has relevance for other groups who gather to further the kingdom. A brief consideration of how women view membership in a congregation will serve, furthermore, to indicate the expectations they bring to other situations.

In the renewal that accompanied Vatican II, sisters examined the structures of authority and obedience and moved away from what are best termed paternalistic forms of government toward participative ones. The notion that leadership and decision-making were the prerogative of the few gave way to the notion of mutual responsibility in equal membership. Principles enunciated at the Council, such as collegiality and subsidiarity, were honored in their Constitutions and translated into their lives. The result has been a burgeoning of leadership, and a wider participation in governance at every level.

Ritual is one means of giving expression to shared values. I participated in one recently which can serve to illustrate the renewed understanding of leadership and authority among women religious.

The occasion was the installation of the prioress general and her four councillors, the women elected to provide leadership for the Sinsinawa Dominican Congregation for the next four years. A former prioress general, who has since returned to high school administration, spoke for the sisters of the congregation. She posed a series of questions to the sisters who had accepted the call to leadership:

> Are you willing to help us discover, appreciate and deepen fundamental gospel values?
>
> Are you willing to render service to each Sister in the full living out of her personal vocation?
>
> Are you willing to remind us of the goals that we have formed together, and exhort us to remain consistently faithful to them?
>
> Are you willing to remind us to make decisions that support and further these goals?

After giving their response, the prioress general and the councillors asked precisely the same questions of all of those present, and each sister came forward to give her answer. The ceremony gave witness to the mutual responsibility we have to one another and to the work of the congregation; each gives and each receives. Those elected to leadership depend on every sister to share in the decision-making process, and to render the same sort of service that she expects of the leaders. The leaders themselves return to educational and pastoral ministry at the end of their terms. This assures a regular renewal of vision and purpose, and prevents the formation of an elite cadre.

At every level of congregation leadership, the role of the one in authority is more to inspire, motivate, and facilitate than to legislate and regulate. Those who hold office are quick to discover the knowledge and skills of others and bring them to the fore. They are equally quick to delegate.

There is not a chasm, then, between those in office and those in the so-called ranks. Each sister knows that she is primarily responsible for her own professional and spiritual development and all know that they share in the responsibility of governance and of mutual support in community.

This model of a congregation whose members are co-responsible for mission corresponds to a vision of church as a community of people who share faith and minister according to their gifts and in response to changing needs. It has been easier, perhaps, for women religious and women in general to affirm this vision. We are less accustomed to, less attracted by, and less attached to notions of privileged rank in rigidly arranged hierarchical structures.

Collaboration between women and men in the church will become easier as the move from church as power structure to church as community becomes more complete. Meanwhile, all will have to make an effort to understand both the limits and the possibilities, the assumptions and the expectations of each. The effort should result in a church that approaches more closely the ideal of a community; one in which the barriers between male and female, cleric and lay, give way to a mutual recognition of personal gifts. Then parish staffs and parishioners, campus ministry teams and students, hospital chaplains and those whom they serve can ask of one another:

Are you willing to help us discover, appreciate and deepen fundamental gospel values?

Are you willing to remind us of the goals that we have formed together, and exhort us to remain consistently faithful to them?

Are you willing to remind us to make decisions that support and further these goals?

And we will begin to enjoy the fruits of mutual ministry.

The Parish Staff

In an attempt to measure to what extent women on parish staffs or teams feel that men and women bring a common vision of ministry to their tasks I engaged several in conversation with leading questions such as, "How do the men and women on your team relate? What have been the opportunities and what the problems or challenges of working together? Is there a sense of equality among team members?

What are the prospects for the future?" Complete equality is precluded, of course, by the automatic restrictions placed on women's ministry, but within those limits what has been women's experience of working more closely with men in parish activities?

A sister serving as Director of Religious Education reflected on her experience in working with priests in two different settings. In neither, she said, was the relationship one of true collaboration. As school principal, she worked independently of the pastor and in collaboration with faculty, parents and the school board. She kept the pastor informed, and was content with his involvement with the school which might be described as one of benign neglect. In her present position she is a member of a parish staff composed of three Order priests, one brother, two deacons, two sisters, and a lay woman who is principal of the grade school. She describes the relationships as hierarchical; the six men at the top, with the pastor at the very top, the three women at the bottom. The pastor brings many gifts to his ministerial role, but lacks administrative skills. Though he chairs all of the meetings, he does not really know how to run one: how to delegate, summarize, move things forward, bring to closure. Ideas presented tend to "plop." The parish council's activities are limited to organizing social functions. The liturgy team goes undirected. Activity at the Sunday eucharist is centered in the sanctuary and the choir loft. "From row 1 to row 50 in the nave, it is b-o-r-i-n-g," she says. Her suggestions about how to involve parish members in ministry, her offer to work with the liturgy team, her desire to expand her own limited role to embrace adult education, the Rite of Christian Initiation for Adults, and religious education in the parish school: all of this falls on deaf ears since too few on the team share her vision of a renewed parish. The two deacons are as clerical in their approach to parish activities as the priests. Decision-making is viewed as the prerogative of the pastor rather than as a process which involves goal definition, creative thinking, and reaction from each staff member. If the hierarchical mold could be broken, other patterns could emerge in this parish allowing a better use of the talents of all. As it is the Director of Religious Education will seek a new ministry in the very near future. She is beginning to wonder if women will ever find full scope for their abilities in institutions or organizations in which men outnumber women and have traditionally exercised power.

It will certainly not be easy for them in the forseeable future, but Dolores Brooks, O.P. has found the effort to collaborate a rewarding one overall. She has been pastoral associate for six years. The other members of the staff are the pastor, two clerical associates, a Religious Education Coordinator and a lay woman school principal. Six years ago neither the staff nor the parishioners had had any experience with women on the parish staff. "It was a minefield," she says, "awkward and sometimes painful." The priests found they had to modify their in-house arrangements and sacrifice some of their privacy. She had to learn to be much more assertive than she ordinarily is. "Men do what they *want* to do; women hesitate and hold back wondering how their desires fit in with everyone else's." Women must act decisively with confidence in their own training and their vision of what a parish can, be. Dolores has a Master's degree in the theology of spirituality and a Master's of Divinity from Weston School of Theology. She still had to make an effort to act on her conviction that she should take responsibility for the mission of the parish. This was true despite the fact that she was educated with women of different faiths who expected to be pastors. "Our social conditioning makes women oversensitive to what *others* want. Men do not hold back," she observes.

Both staff and parishioners, two-thirds of them women, extended a warm welcome to Dolores. The parish is open and accepts persons on their merit and their ability to provide spiritual leadership. Dolores' main role has been to facilitate lay leadership, a task she enjoys and one that sisters have played an important role in developing.

What have been the hindrances to collaborative ministry? Dolores sees the limit imposed on her sacramental and liturgical role as the main one. She acts as lector, eucharistic minister, and occasionally as homilist. She presides at certain non-eucharistic functions, especially in Advent and Lent. But since the Sunday liturgy is at the heart of parish life, she feels keenly the limitations placed on her part in it.

The restrictions frustrate her hospital ministry, too. Having walked with the sick through a journey which would end most naturally in her ministration of the sacraments of reconciliation or anointing, she must stop short. This sacramental ministry is the domain of the three ordained members of the staff.

What are the possibilities for collaboration in the future? "This will depend," says Dolores, "on the clarity of focus of the women who enter pastoral ministry." Her advice to those who plan to do so is to examine the parish structure closely. If it becomes clear that they will not be able to share equally in basic decision-making and planning, they should move on. "The staff has to model shared ministry or it won't happen in the parish," she observes. Women should not look to the staff, however, to fulfill their every personal need. They should have many resources outside the parish and the parish staff. "Men offer little emotional support," she observes, "and if women expect it they will be disappointed."

Dolores believes women have a unique contribution to make to the realization of collaborative ministry, both at the parish and the diocesan levels, but their resources for spiritual leadership have hardly been tapped.

Change is occurring slowly. More parish staffs are supporting women, including them in liturgical functions and in the decision-making process. Women continue to raise consciousness about what remains to be done. Dolores herself is not always patient with the pace of change, but reminds herself that it is emotionally and experientially difficult to alter old patterns. We are all caught in structures of tradition and education which blind us to inequities and to new possibilities. The fact that her parish and parish staff recognize the problems and struggle to overcome them gives her hope.

An Alternative Model

Women religious and priests or brothers played the dominant roles in the collaborative efforts considered so far. The St. Giles Family Mass Community in Oak Park, Illinois offers a model where lay women and men take responsibility for every aspect of their "parish within a parish." The Community is composed of about 95 core families or 300 people, including children who are an important part of the Community. The families organized the Community eleven years ago since traditional parish structures did not offer the kind of liturgy, catechesis, or community they were searching for. They maintain their membership in the larger parish, however, and value their connection with it since they do not want to become a kind of sect.

The women and men of the Community work together on the Community Council, the pastoral team, the liturgy planning committee, the catechetical team, the finance committee, and the Priest Search Committee. The relationship of equal partners which they have established in their marriages carries over to their work in the Community.

Kathleen Sullivan-Stewart points out that negotiating male/female relationships on several fronts has a reinforcing effect. Community members interact as husband and wife, as co-workers, and as family members. What happens in one arena can be discussed and analyzed in the other. The attempt to raise children in non-sexist ways, for instance, and the reminders parents get from children when they fail or even falter in this regard, can affect not only the distribution of household duties but also the assigning of liturgical roles.

The harmonizing of male and female systems in the Community was not the work of a day, however, and it is not complete. Women originally organized the Community, and the assumptions that underlie it are those of equality, consensus, and cooperation. It was not easy for men used to a chain of command and the structures of the corporate world to adapt to the female context, and to work with vocal women whose training in theology, liturgy, and catechesis was superior to their own. In a strange reversal of roles, men in the Community began to resent the position of the women and to assert that, given a chance, they could do as well as their female counterparts. The women, on the other hand, feared that men would take over if given a chance, and that the responsiveness and lightness of structure would be transfomred into deadening formality. "In fact," says Pat Junius, "there is a joke in the Community that asks 'When did we get into trouble?' to which the answer is 'When we began to apply Roberts

Rules.'" Kathleen Sullivan-Stewart observes that the
diffuse and informal system, however, had problems
not only for men, but for some women, too. "If
nothing else," she says, "structure has given us a
common language for fighting over things. It has also
provided focus and made it easier to turn over jobs
and to communicate." Peter Junius thinks that it has
become possible within the Community to honestly
respect individual expertise, and to move away from
categories which separate men and women into cold
organizers, on the one hand, and warm empathizers
on the other. Pat Sikorski agrees. "Men have learned
to 'mother'," she says, "and have been freed to touch
more easily and cry."

Now men and women serve in equal numbers on
the pastoral team and the Community Council. A
woman and man serve as co-ordinators of the "Town
Hall," the assembly of the Community gathered to
hammer out policies and group decisions. Women
administer and make policies for the Liturgy Round
Table and the cathetical program, but both men and
women serve as catechists and liturgy planners. The
cooperation of men and women on the Priest Search
Committee gave proof, if any was needed, that it was
possible to work hard together as equal members of a
well-coordinated team. The committee drew up
guidelines, found and interviewed candidates, and
selected a priest celebrant for the Community.

What is the role of the priest in a community in
which lay members do everything from preparation
for the sacraments to the administration of finances?

"He is one among many," answers Sullivan-Stewart. "He presides at the eucharist as the priest celebrant, but the community co-celebrates." And what they are celebrating is the eucharist as sign of God already and always present in the community. As member of the pastoral team, the priest celebrant's activities do not differ from those of the other members of the team, and he does not exercise any special authority. On the other hand he shares in the life of the community. He is not a cultic figure who appears once a week to "confect the eucharist."

Over the years the establishment of a peer relationship between priest and lay people has required a mutual effort. The first priest associated with the community had no difficulty in accepting women in the traditional role of catechist, for instance, but resisted at first their leadership in pastoral and liturgical functions. Fr. Paul Bechtold, the third priest celebrant who has served the community, found that his one-year experience deepened his understanding of certain aspects of priesthood. "I learned to take the role of priest as servant very seriously," he said, "and to be servant is to listen attentively." In the liturgy he responded to the concerns of the Community as voiced through the planning committee, and although he did not consider himself a slave of the committee, he generally went in the direction they indicated.

Although the Community offers an admirable way of being church, Fr. Bechtold does not anticipate that the model will become a common one in parish life.

It demands high levels of good will and of professional competency, as well as an enormous investment of time and of self. Where lay people are willing to make the commitment, priesthood by baptism and the ordained priesthood come visibly into right relationship. "We have an ordained priesthood," said Fr. Bechtold, "because we have a baptized people."

The Community of St. Giles offers an example of an assembly gathered as people of God. They struggle to overcome barriers between the sexes, between clerical and lay, and between classes. The community gathers in a kind of extended family, parents and children, singles, single parents, divorced men and women, and people from every point on the economic spectrum. Those in financial need can request loans or grants from the emergency fund, and the wealthier members of the Community often find ways to give further anonymous help to members in need. "Fences are low in the community," says Pat Sikorski. "We feel responsible for one another. Being part of the community means not only worshiping together, but allowing people to know you, to enter your life, to share hurts, and joys, and needs." A seven-year-old community member, when asked how the community Mass in the parish gym differed from Mass in church put it this way, "Well, we take off our coats, and we call each other by name, and we talk together about important things."

This building of community and, therefore of the Kingdom, has required the courage to look beyond conventional structures. The willingness to do so has

had happy results: members, women and men, succeed one another in leadership positions, all participate in decisions affecting the Community, and
the sacramental and prayer life of all has been im-
mensely enriched. Co-laboring to build the local
church has, furthermore, proved to be an effective
antidote to the alienation experienced by so many in
modern American cities and suburbs.

Prospects for the Future

Will collaborative ministry become the rule rather
than the exception in tomorrow's church? Does it
face an embattled future? What steps can men and
women take to assure its success?

I posed these questions to Diane Kennedy, O.P.,
who has given serious thought to the question of collaborative ministry. She served as Director of the
Parable Conference from 1976-1982. The Conference
is the only organization in the United States which
has explicitly addressed the question of collaboration. Its organizers have done so because true collaboration among members of the Order is a means
of attaining Parable's end: renewal of the life and
mission of the Dominican Order in the service of the
church.

Diane and her co-worker, Carmelita Murphy, O.P.
are hopeful about the future of collaborative
ministry, but are not naive about the difficulties men
and women face in establishing it. Some who
sincerely want to participate in new models of col-

laboration are blind to the obstacles they place in its way. "Movement from blindness to sight," writes Diane, "can happen only by finding appropriate structures of communication that will develop understanding of difference and gradually build a shared vision of ministry."[13]

Carmelita Murphy in her thesis entitled *Collaboration of Women and Men in Christian Life and Ministry* underscores the deeply entrenched habits of mind that make it difficult for priests to see women, lay and religious, take charge, question men's decisions, offer them spiritual direction, or otherwise step out of expected behavior. On the other hand, capable women sometimes hide behind a facade of submission and exercise their influence in indirect and manipulative ways. Still, the Parable directors are confident that ministry in tomorrow's church will be the domain of women and men working together as equals.

Diane observes that old structures remain, but the foundations are gone. "A whole new form of life is emerging," she contends, "which will push out those structures." The new forms of collaboration will include lay, religious, and clergy in imaginative combinations. Parable retreats and conferences for Dominican religious and laity offer models for the kind of collaboration that will be common in the future in various church settings.

A Parable retreat brings together Dominican men and women, lay and religious, both as directors and as participants. Two priests and two sisters ordinarily direct the retreat. All four preach, serve as retreat directors, plan the liturgy, and assess the movement of the retreat. The women on the team play a visible role during the liturgy, sometimes leading the penitential rite, fractioning the bread with the priest, offering the prayer of the faithful, or giving the homily. There is only one main celebrant; priests making the retreat join others in the pews. Throughout the retreat the directors and participants relate as equals with diverse gifts. In the summer of 1982 the first lay woman served as a retreat director, adding a new and welcome dimension to the collaborative model.

The encouragement of American bishops augurs well for this sort of collaboration of men and women, religious, clergy and lay. Archbishop Weakland of Milwaukee in a pastoral letter entitled "Shared Gifts, Shared Responsibility" makes the point that collaboration cannot remain a theological theorem, but must become a Christian lifestyle. And Diane is fond of quoting Bishop Murphy of Baltimore:

> [Collaboration] involves an ability to include others even when you may be working or thinking alone. It requires a conviction that one's work and thought and even one's life will be enhanced by claiming the blessings that come only by way of the perspectives and efforts of other people.[14]

Blessings there certainly will be, and a more adequate response to the needs of church and society.

Meanwhile, there will also be confusion, conflict, tension, and hard work, the inevitable companions of growth and renewal. Women can expect that opposition will harden in certain quarters as they come closer to the goal of a fair share in decision-making at all levels.

But there are strong trends visible in the church, and there is reasonable hope that men and women, clergy and lay, will continue to relate in new ways, shed fears of losing old powers, and come to a new understanding of the role of authority in community. Women have a central role to play in strengthening the currents moving in this direction.

Chapter Five

FEMINISM AND AMERICAN CATHOLIC WOMEN

THE buttons that proclaim "Jesus was a Feminist" may not be as shocking today as when people first sported them some eight or nine years ago. But there are still those who wonder if one can be at the same time a Christian and a feminist. Is there a basic contradiction between feminism and Christianity? Is Christianity inherently anti-woman? Or is there in Christianity a radical message of freedom which extends logically to women, even if the institutional church has consistently failed to apply it fully to us?

Neither Christianity, nor Catholicism, nor feminism are simple realities. Each has a history, a worldview, and a philosophy. And the adherents to any one of the three systems of thought run the full gamut from radical to conservative. Trying to see how they relate to one another is an intricate affair. While I have no doubt that Christianity and feminism are, at the very least, compatible, it would be foolish to deny that believers in both camps have eyed one another suspiciously, and even condemned one another roundly. Some feminists insist that the stories and symbols of religion have had more to do with keeping us subordinate than any other factor in the course of human history. They point out that women's position is lowest in countries where the Catholic church's position is the strongest: Italy and

Spain. They proclaim that organized religion is inherently sexist, and that women will not be free until we reject it. If certain feminists in the past and present have looked on the church as enemy, some churchmen have returned the favor in kind. Many were found in the past and are still to be found who agree with an editor of the last century who wrote of women's "clamorous and unfeminine declaration of personal rights which it is obvious Providence never destined them to exercise." He was referring to his female co-workers who claimed the right to organize in labor unions. Today God is invoked as the final obstacle in the attainment of other rights women seek in and out of the church, the right, for instance, to have the call to priesthood tested.

Meanwhile feminists within the churches are looking with new eyes at scripture, theology, and ethics. While exposing the inadequacy of male-centered and male-oriented thought in these areas, they are broadening the horizons of religious studies, enriching and revitalizing the length and breadth of the Judeo-Christian tradition.

Before considering how feminism has affected thought by and about women in the American Catholic church, it will be useful to set the women's movement in historical perspective and to examine some of its basic insights.

Basic Insights of the Feminist Movement

The women's movement is not a homogeneous,

highly organized movement with goals easily defined and agreed upon by all. We can distinguish feminists who want to share power with men in the existing system from those who want to radically re-structure societal institutions; Christian feminists from goddess-worshipping feminists; radical lesbian separatists from straight feminists; Marxist socialist feminists from those in the political mainstream. The attempt to characterize the movement and to set forth its fundamental assumptions is, therefore, risky and the result is bound to be incomplete. If I undertake the task here, it is simply to give some idea of the seriousness and the scope of the movement and to suggest why growing numbers of American Catholic women support it.

The question of identity is the basic one of the women's movement. All other issues are contingent on this one: what constitutes being a woman (or man) in our society?

The seemingly innocent question is really an explosive one, and the movement has been justly called a revolution, the most profound revolution since the French one in the late 18th century. Indeed, in order to see the women's movement correctly, it should be viewed as part of the same deep-running historical trend which sparked the French revolution. John Stuart Mill characterizes this trend as a movement away from moralities of command and obedience and toward a morality of real justice.[1] In line with this movement successive subordinate groups have challenged the power exercised over them by a dominant, controlling group. The divisions were, and are,

evident in the categories of class, race and gender:
rulers and ruled, white and black, male and female.
The unequal status of these various groups enjoyed
the sanction of classical Greek and Roman thought,
the church Fathers, and legal and economic systems
down the ages. Because the privileged groups found
the arrangements handy, they strengthened them by
presenting them as natural, and even as ordained by
God.

One of the more dramatic challenges to class
distinctions came in the French Revolution. Our own
civil war in the last century, and the civil rights
movements and colonial uprisings in the present
one, have made inroads on white supremacy. These
movements were accompanied to some extent or
followed by an ever intensified consciousness on the
part of women of a system of sexual caste.

In this system male-dominance is the cultural
norm and men are considered to be the creative,
authority-bearing, justice-dispensing agents. Women
are the passive, subservient agents, whose lives
derive meaning from their relations to men. Their
most essential task, and the one that best defines
them, is child-bearing. Men in this system enjoy
superior status in the family, state, and church.
Women defer to them and are generally in secondary
and service positions, doing the repetitive and
behind-the-scenes tasks.

American women first organized to challenge this
system at a meeting held in a Methodist church at
Seneca Falls, New York in July, 1848. Feminists of

the 20th century have been amazed to discover the depth of the analysis done by these foremothers whose thought and achievements have occupied so little space in history texts. Much of the force and breadth of the original thinkers and organizers of the movement was sacrificed as energy was channeled into a fight for women's suffrage. That battle won, the organized movement lost focus and momentum until the early 60's. At this point, consciousness-raising groups with minimal organization, as well as the highly-structured National Organization of Women took up where the first wave of feminism left off.

Since then feminist theory has forced a re-examination in almost every field of knowledge: history, literature, theology, biology, economics, linguistics, medicine, law, and psychology among others. But the revolution has not been limited to the halls of academe. Women have created a social ferment as well by asking aloud questions which they had scarcely dared to think previously, or which they raised only sporadically and in whispers. Since the questions touch on such fundamental and sensitive issues as ego-concept, personhood, marriage, work, sex roles, power and money, it is not surprising that the revolution is not yet over. Indeed, it has hardly begun.

Still we have already learned some lessons. What has the movement taught us? Basically, to question and reject sex roles which assign the genders a certain set of characteristics and intellectual traits which cast the sexes as opposites. The traits assigned to women range from compassion, nurturance, and intuition to the less desirable ones of incompetence, fickleness, immaturity, and emotionalism. This assignment presumably justifies the subsequent assignment of separate social conventions and functions, economic position, standards of behavior, and degree of access to education, the professions, independence, health, wealth, and leisure. The women's movement has unveiled the damaging effects on us and on the human race in general of a world thus divided, a world which robs women of our history, deprives us of our names, ignores or belittles our achievements, drains us of self-confidence, and demands twice as much of us as of males to win recognition; a world in which women of independent thought and action are often punished; a world in which so-called women's work is considered trivial and is ill-paid, if paid at all.

Feminists have not only exposed the injustices of the social and economic order, but at another and deeper level have suggested the rewards that await women who join in the quest for transcedence. The search requires that women refuse definition in terms of biological function and reject an image of woman as static, hidden, and selfless. It requires seeing ourselves as unique, developing persons who are self-possessed, self-creating, self-defining, strong, and active. Women are moving toward this awareness, but the struggle is far from over.

Hélène Cixous, a French feminist writer, gives

voice to the energy and creativity of women, on the one hand, and to the hesitation and climate of expectation, on the other, which sap our spirit and energy:

> I, too, overflow; my desires have invented new desires, my body knows unheard of songs. Time and again I have felt so full of luminous desires that I could burst—burst with forms much more beautiful than those which are put up in frames and sold for a stinking fortune. And I...said nothing...I was afraid...I said to myself: You are mad! Where is the ebullient, infinite woman who...led into self-disdain by the great arm of...phallocentrism, hasn't been ashamed of her strength? Who, surprised and horrified by the fantastic tumult of her drives (for she was made to believe that a...normal woman has a divine composure), hasn't accused herself of being a monster? Who, feeling a funny desire...(to sing, to write, to dare to speak, in short, to bring out something new) hasn't thought she was sick?[2]

Many women are familiar with these phenomena: the creative self in doubt, health mistaken for sickness, potential achievement for monstrosity. And many, like Cixous, are beginning to see, to break the silence, and to write themselves into the text.

This unleashing of women's spirit has been one of the fruits of the women's movement. Women are discovering that the act of creating progressively opens our being, revealing deeper and deeper levels of its possibilities. But the effort often requires an initial mental revolution. Tillie Olsen speaks of the

inequities, restrictions, penalties, denials and
leechings which have to be faced and conquered if
women are to create. She speaks of how small girls
are denied the development of their human endow-
ment: active, vigorous bodies, exercise of the power
to do, to make, to investigate, to invent, to conquer
obstacles, to resist violations of the self, to think,
choose, to attain community and confidence in self.[3]

The two decades since the rebirth of the women's
movement has helped women reclaim all of this.
Through the writings of Millett, De Beauvoir,
Daly, Olsen, Ehrenreich, Chesler, Janeway, Fire-
stone, Rich, Morgan, Carroll, and many others we've
learned to re-read the past; we've learned to face
unpleasant truths without imagining that we are
determined by them; we've learned how to see
through myths which devalue women; we've learned
to stop laughing at jokes which are at our expense.
We're now searching for, and finding, myths which
speak to us. We're putting to rest the Terrible Mother
(castrating bitch) and the Good Mother (nurturer and
comforter)—myths which define us only in terms of
men's needs and men's fears. We're learning to reject
what hampers us in our attempt to understand and
value ourselves in terms of our *own* being, our fundamental identity as an autonomous self.

The movement has yielded insights which go
beyond woman's selfhood, however. Awareness of
sexual polarity has sharpened awareness of other
false oppositions: those between work and play,
mind and imagination, action and contemplation,

flesh and spirit, nature and nurture. At the level of social conflict, the dissection of the oppression of women has furnished insights into the exploitative mentality at work in other arenas, those, namely, of race, class, and national interest. It can be argued, indeed, that sexism is the most fundamental oppression since the way men and women relate in society is a prime determinant in the whole social system. Perhaps only when patterns of domination and subjugation are eliminated on this level, will liberation at other levels be possible.

In seeing the duality of the sexes as a paradigm for other polarities, and perhaps even as the basis for them, feminists are not suggesting that the latter are ineradicable since the fact of two sexes will not go away. We cannot, and would not want to if it were possible, eliminate the biological fact of two sexes. That is not the problem. As Janeway points out, the problem is the unequal assignment of value and importance to masculine and feminine gender.[4] At another level, the problem is the division of personhood that results from assigning to women and men roles and patterns of behavior that deprive both of full humanity. When that very basic division is overcome, we will be better able to move beyond patriarchal oppositions in search of greater harmony within the human community and with nature itself.

We will be able to build intellectual frameworks and human relations that look beyond either-or, true-false, good-bad, superior-inferior, strong-weak, conquering and conquered. And those traits which have

been considered a female specialty and relegated to
the private sphere may be looked upon as desirable
for all and find their place in the public sphere: con-
servation, the nurturing of life, mercy, compassion,
and careful attention to person.

Feminism and Catholicism

The insights of the women's movement have not
been lost on American Catholic women. From the
beginning it was clear to many that a transformed
female consciousness would require a transformation in theology, ethics, interpretation of scripture,
liturgy, ministry and church structures. They have
joined other Christian and Jewish women in a
feminist critique of religious ideologies and symbols
and in the search for new formulations which take
into account women's re-reading of ourselves and of
the patriarchal past. They have also joined together
in organizations and coalitions whose aim is to
reflect and to develop strategies for transforming the
church in ways that will allow for the realization of
female autonomy.

Feminist Critique And Vision

As feminists unveiled the mechanisms of oppression in the political, social, and economic realms,
scholars within the religious traditions began to
discover, examine, and reject sexist assumptions in
church teachings and policies. Mary Daly in *The*

Church and the Second Sex was one of the first to
expose the pervasive misogynism of the Fathers of
the Church, and to demonstrate the reinforcing effect that church thought and teaching has had on the
unequal status of the sexes. It proved a simple task to
unearth depressing texts which protrayed women as
weak-willed, concupiscent, dangerous, and dull.
Woman was commonly associated with body, car-
nality, and evil, while man was considered to typify
spirit, virtue, and mind. Women would find their
salvation in obedience and service to the more
reasonable, controlled, and intelligent males and in
their role as childbearer. This tendency to define
women in a subordinate relation to men and prin-
cipally in terms of their capacity to reproduce long
outlasted patristic times. It runs counter to woman's
experience of herself as an individual whose
selfhood has meaning and a destiny beyond those
assigned by wifehood and motherhood. But women's
search for the transcendent is severely handicapped
in the Judeo-Christian tradition which has been
shaped by men's experience and expressed through
men's symbols and stories.

Carol P. Christ, among others, has underlined the
necessity for women to "seek, discover, and create
the symbols, metaphors, and plots of our own
experience."[5] That experience is absent from the
language of myth and sacred story. Until now men
have told the stories of men and women alike, and
women are obliged to read themselves sidewise into
stories of fathers and sons. The one-dimensional

male perception of ultimate power and reality not only alienates women, but robs religious traditions of the richness that full human experience would provide. As women become more capable of giving voice to their own experience, as they recover and affirm their authentic female identities, religious thought and language are gradually being transformed, new perceptions of being and of becoming are opening out, and new modes of thinking about the ultimate are taking shape.

The attempt to re-read scripture, to transform religious language, to forge new symbols, and to expand the possibilities for spiritual discovery for women within the Judeo-Christian tradition is based on the conviction that this tradition is not inherently sexist. Not all feminists share that conviction. Mary Daly and Naomi Goldenberg, among others, have abandoned the task of reforming or transforming traditional theologies and have continued the spiritual quest outside organized religions. Some have sought in a return to goddess worship the identity and power denied them by church fathers .

A growing body of literature explores the possibilities of a new women's spirituality outside the confines of patriarchal religions. Charlene Spretnak brings together provocative essays in *The Politics of Women's Spirituality*.[6] The contributors to this volume are in basic agreement that a symbol system based on a male divinity makes it difficult, if not impossible, for women to conceive of themselves as created in God's image. A woman, writes Carol P. Christ:

may see herself as like God...only by denying her own sexual identity and affirming God's transcendence of sexual identity. But she can never have the experience that is freely available to every man and boy in her culture, of having her full sexual identity affirmed as being in the image and likeness of God.[7]

Male power and authority seem natural against the background of this symbol system, while female power is suspect or non-existent. Women are reduced to seeking salvation in and through males, and fail to find in themselves the saving and healing powers of strength and wisdom which have their roots in the divine. In remembering and honoring female deities of the Great Goddess, on the other hand, increasing numbers of women are finding access to new spiritual and personal power and an effective key to female independence and strength.

Women are not the sole beneficiaries of feminist spirituality. The values which permeate it are those of union, harmony, creative process, responsiveness, and nurturance as against those of separation, struggle, destruction, war, competition, and conquest. The reclaiming of female power will mean not a reversal of roles nor a vindictive repression, but the creation of new modes of thinking and of relating, a new concept of power, and new possibilities of integration. Those only need fear it who are blindly attached to hierarchical divisions, exploitative uses of power, and the continued devaluation and denigration of women.

Is it necessary to step outside of the Judeo-

Christian tradition to reclaim female power and the
strength of female bonds? Is the system irredeemably
patriarchal? Or is it possible to be at once a feminist
and a Christian? The questions are crucial for
women who recognize fully the validity of the
feminist critique of Christian theology and sym-
bolism, and who yet find in the tradition a meaningful framework for dealing with fear, loss, pain,
and death, and a basis for hope, reconciliation,
peace, justice, and community. Christian feminist
theologians are struggling with the questions and
providing some of the most exciting and provocative
insights of contemporary theology. Anne Carr points
out that their work is not peripheral to theological
thought, but constitutes an intrinsic theological task.
Unlike theologies of play, hope, or work, which
require the application of a Christian perspective to
contemporary issues, feminist theology "implies not
only a Christian critique of sexist or patriarchal
culture but a feminist critique of Christianity."[8]

The realization that the Christian tradition has
always been subject to new interpretation, and has
always been influenced by historical and cultural
factors, puts the current feminist critique into
perspective. To remain alive, Christianity must
respond in our day to women's new self-concept,
questions, search, and vision, as it has responded in
the past to changing concepts of social and political
organization.

The work of feminist theologians proceeds on
several fronts. They are moving beyond the exposi-

tion of sexist distortions of the past and searching for
tools and methodologies which will break through
the limitations of androcentric theologies. They are
speaking in a language which takes women's experience into account. They are searching for images
and symbols which will affirm women as well as
men, and make it easier for women to recognize and
affirm the divine in ourselves. They are reinter-
preting myths from women's point of view. They are
re-examining notions of sin and grace from female
points of reference. The object is not to create a "For
Women Only" theology, but to include the lives,
being, and experience of half the human race into the
human task of theologizing. By refusing to accept
sexist parameters of traditional theologies, feminist
theologians are pushing theological thought toward
wholeness. For as they help eliminate barriers to
women's sense of autonomy and self-transcendence,
they open the way to new and more egalitarian relationships within the entire human community.
Margaret Farley's essay "New Patterns of Relationship: Beginnings of a Moral Revolution"[9] can serve
to illustrate some of the themes, the direction, and
the possibilities of Christian feminist thought. Farley
argues that whether or not male/female relationships
have changed significantly, they *ought* to change
because on the whole they have prevented individual
growth, given rise to social injustices, and failed to
conform to Christ's teachings. She then looks
through a woman's lens at the notions of Christian
love and justice and finds that the equal regard, self-

sacrifice, and mutuality which are meant to characterize Christian love become problematic in Christian thought when applied to love for a person precisely as woman or man. Neither equal regard nor mutuality is possible when woman is considered essentially subordinate to man; and the meaning of self-sacrifice, attributed in a particular way to women, is falsified when it is linked to a pattern of submissiveness to men.

In her elaboration of the theme of self-sacrifice, Farley enters into a nuanced discussion of the notions of activity and receptivity as they apply to Christian agape, and to the new understanding women have reached of their own bodies and of their expectations of love. She makes clear the relationship between a true understanding of Christian agape and women's understanding of love as something "...which is utterly receptive and utterly active, a communion in which the beloved is received and affirmed, in which receiving and giving are but two sides of one reality which is other-centered love."[10] The danger, of course, is that theologians will persist in identifying women with this sort of love (and men with knowledge) thereby denying to both the full benefits of Christian agape. This section demonstrates admirably the false problems raised by a theology based on misunderstandings of sexual identity and the human person. The central Christian concept of love of God and neighbor has suffered from a tendency to equate the active principle with God and maleness and the passive or receptive principle with femaleness, thus dividing what should be joined in integral love and communion.

Development of the element of mutuality in Christian love gives Farley the opportunity to grapple with the symbol of the Trinity as Father, Son, and Holy Spirit. No Christian feminist can avoid confronting the issue of an exclusive male God since Mary Daly raised it in *Beyond God the Father*. In that book Daly demonstrates how the Christian symbol system, with God the Father at its center, has served to justify and sustain a social system oppressive to women. Farley agrees that Christian theology, insofar as it has failed to attribute to women the fullness of the image of God, has erected barriers to women's equality. She then explores the possibilities of naming the First Person Mother as well as Father, the Second Person Daughter as well as Son, but moves beyond the ideas expressed in parent/child relationships to an image better able to express the notions of equality and mutuality: God as symbol of the love between man and woman. She asks:

> Is it not possible...to describe the First Person as masculine and the Second Person as feminine and the bond which is the infinite communion between them (the Spirit of both) as necessarily both masculine and feminine? Do we not have here revealed a relationship in which both the First Person and the Second Person are infinitely active and infinitely receptive, infinitely giving and infinitely receiving, holding in infinite mutuality and reciprocity a totally shared life?[11]

It would be equally possible, of course, to describe the First Person (the generative principle) as feminine and the Second Person as masculine, and perhaps more fitting to do so. In any case, it is important to remember that no image fully mirrors God's reality. The point in introducing an explicitly female principle in the Christian symbol for God is not to replace one inadequate symbol with another, one which will take on in its turn the illusion of objective reality. The point is to recognize the limitations of the symbol of God the Father and Son, and to acknowledge the barriers that it has placed to women's ability to see ourselves as images of God, creative, powerful, and wise. The point is to image God in many ways and in ways likely to render visible and desirable patterns of human relationship which are marked by total equality and reciprocity. Jesus' image of the kingdom of God as a mustard seed did not rule out the image of the kingdom as a woman searching for a lost coin, nor as a man casting a net into the sea. It is imperative that we distance ourselves from the single, outmoded image of the patriarchal Supreme Being and that we continue to search for images of God which reflect her many faces, which affirm the selfhood of each individual, and which model mutual rather than hierarchical ways of relating. Christian feminists will continue to enrich this search in ways which will not only enhance women's personhood and validate our spiritual quest, but will humanize the whole theological enterprise. The recognition of women and women's values opens the way for the inclusion of the viewpoint of other oppressed groups with whom we have much in common.

Feminist Strategy and Action

When change or revolution at the level of thought and analysis is profound, change at the level of structure and institution is inevitable. The connections between Enlightenment thought and the French Revolution, or between Marxist analysis and socialist revolutions are strong and obvious. Those between the feminist critique (which began systematically in the 19th century) and the changed position of women in terms of the law, education, work, family, and church are not less so. Other forces have been at work, of course, but the impact of the feminist movement cannot be discounted. The relationship is not so much one of single cause and effect. It is rather a more subtle one of mutual reinforcement. In regard to feminism in the church, Elizabeth Schüssler-Fiorenza points out that changes in theological language and imagery will not succeed unless institutions change in ways that support the insights born of Christian feminism. But changes in structure and practice will be neither far-reaching nor permanent as long as theological imagery and myth serve to maintain women's inferior status.[12]

Women have joined together in several organizations in the church to work for the translation into institutional structures of the intellectual revolution that has taken place in regard to gender identity and role. Once touched by this revolution, women find painful what had, perhaps, seemed natural before their awakening. They can no longer accept male-fixated language, anti-woman church positions, unjust wages, homilies and religious education which reinforce sexist stereotypes, or attitudes and behavior which ignore, trivialize, exclude, or suggest condescension toward women. While struggling against all of this, women are taking positive steps toward consciousness-raising at all levels, and toward the creation of a church in which women's problems are recognized, our insights valued, and our talents given full scope. National and local organizations have provided forums and support networks for these women. Their conferences, publications, and resolutions keep women's issues alive. They help to create a feeling of solidarity among women in the church, and lend weight and force to women's efforts to obtain justice. It will be useful here to indicate the nature and scope of some of these organizations.

National Assembly of Religious Women

This group was founded in 1970 as the National Assembly of Women Religious. The name change, effected in August 1982, reflects the organization's reach to include not only women in religious con-gregations but all "... religious feminist women committed to the prophetic tasks of giving witness, raising awareness, and engaging in public action for the achievement of justice."[13] The inclusion of two lay members on the National Board indicates the growing importance of lay participation. The Assembly enjoys an individual membership of 1,500 and thirty-five Sisters' Councils or Senates. NARW's National Coordinator, Marjorie Tuite, O.P., describes the organization as multi-issued. "But whether we consider peace, poverty, refugees, or farm workers we highlight women's concerns and look through a feminist lens," she says. The concern for a wide range of social issues, and the clear focus on women's position, mark all of NARW's activities: workshops, the Citizen Action Network, programs materials, and the national bi-monthly publication *Probe.* The latter is an excellent resource for women who share NARW's vision goal of "doing theology as women of faith, using social analysis as a tool for change, acting collectively to build peace with justice." Recent issues have explored the themes of bonding, sexism in the church, women's work, the feminization of poverty, and feminism and militarism. The pages speak eloquently of women's oppression, presenting the social facts which document it and calling for political action and public policy advocacy to overcome it.

While emphasizing women's issues, NARW continually points out the connections between racism, classism, sexism and ageism. The justice commitment of its members extends to all: refugees, immigrant workers, the elderly, battered women, and victims of economic exploitation here and abroad. Marjorie Tuite challenges the members to give voice to that commitment by adopting a prophetic stance and speaking a prophetic word.[14] Convinced that the revolutionary climate of a country is determined by the political awareness of women, Marjorie calls upon women to claim the prophet's role, to name oppression boldly, to grieve with the oppressed, and to build a foundation for hope by helping to create alternatives in health care, in housing, in schools, in the workplace, in decision-making and in ways of relating. NARW plays an important role in bringing women together to explore these issues. At national meetings and conferences and at local workshops, members exchange information, develop strategies, learn organizing skills, and support one another in the attempt to translate social analysis into action. The spirit that informs NARW combines a tough, practical, political realism with a vision of faith and hope rooted in the gospel. It is a spirit that sustains the women in the organization who continue to critique political, legal, economic and religious institutions in their struggle "for the achievement of justice."

National Coalition of American Nuns

NCAN was born at a meeting of sisters in Chicago in the summer of 1969. They had come together to develop "Survival Strategies for the Seventies." One of the speakers at that meeting was Mary Daly. The first action NCAN took was to support Mary Daly's fight for tenure at Boston College. Since then the group has persistently pursued its goal of "studying, working and speaking out on issues related to human rights and social justice." The organization of NCAN is simpler in its structure than that of NARW. The latter operates through fourteen regions which provide representatives to the National Board. NCAN operates through a Board of 24 sisters, whose membership is renewed through nominations made by Board members. The latter meet annually to set priorities for the year. All board members are encouraged to speak out in the name of NCAN on the highlighted issues or any issue related to the principles agreed upon by the Board. Margaret Traxler, SSND and Donna Quinn, O.P., have been two of the most outspoken Board members. They are quick to identify issues and to speak boldly on behalf of victims of injustice, whether these be women in the church, Soviet Jews, political dissidents, or migrant families.

NCAN does not pretend to be a grassroots organization. Its membership of 1800 constitutes only about two percent of American nuns, although many of its positions are supported by a much larger percentage. The size of the organization permits it to move swiftly on controversial issues and to to take action while the outcome of certain decisions can still be influenced.

Like NARW, NCAN has spoken out on a variety of social justice issues. A strong feminist strain runs

through many of the stances adopted by the group.
In the early 70's it spoke out against the interference
by certain bishops in the sisters' renewal protest.
Today it charges that Canon Law's provisions in
regard to women religious are immoral because they
represent rule without consent of the governed.
NCAN has supported ratification of the ERA and
women's ordination, and has bravely confronted
educational, ecclesial, and governmental institutions
that have discriminated against women. In April
1982, the organization issued a statement on abortion which nuanced the simple "ban abortion" position of pro-life groups (see Chapter 3). It can usually
be counted on to support marginalized groups which
less independent organizations tend to shun. It was
the first Catholic organization to publicly support
New Ways Ministry, a group which explores the experience of the Catholic homosexual. And as early as
1978, NCAN called for the de-criminalization of
prostitution, recognizing the need of women engaged in it for certain social and civil benefits denied
them.

NCAN's *Newsletter* keeps its readers informed on
current events in regard to women's rights, workers'
rights, prison issues, disarmament, and nuclear pro-
liferation. It often calls its membership to action:
letter-writing, participation in boycotts, leafletting,
picketing, demonstrating. Its tone is aggressive, and
sometimes delightfully irreverent. Through its
Newsletter and frequent public statements and
actions, NCAN plays an important role in the strug-

gle to secure justice for all within the Church and in society.

Women's Ordination Conference

WOC channels its energies toward the accomplishment of a single goal: the ordination of Roman Catholic women to a renewed priestly ministry. The emphasis on the renewal of ordained priesthood is as important as the entrance of women into that ministry. The Conference, while calling for an end to the discrimination which bars women from ordination, calls simultaneously for an end to models of leadership marked by elitism and by a refusal to share responsibility and decision-making. It reminds women that they must bring with them to ordination a strong commitment to the poor and to minorities, and a determination to challenge patterns of dominance/dependence wherever they exist. The Conference grew out of the efforts of a small group of lay women and women religious brought together in Chicago at the invitation of Mary B. Lynch in 1974. This Task Force planned the conference "Women in Future Priesthood Now: A Call to Action" held in Detroit in November 1975, and helped implement the proposal introduced there that a national organization be formed. By March 1976, the principles, organizational model, and tasks of the national WOC had been agreed upon. By June of the same year a nineteen-member Core Commission had been selected. One of WOC's first lobbying efforts

took place at the Bishops Centennial Call to Action in
October 1976. At first denied delegate status, the
Conference challenged the Credential Committee,
attained delegate status, and went on to take a leader-
ship role in formulating recommendations on
"Women in the Church."

While planning a second major conference, the
Core Commission of WOC maintained dialogue with
Bishops, attempted to identify women who are called
to priesthood, as well as schools and seminaries willing to prepare women for ordination, and initiated
discussion groups throughout the country on the
topic of women and men's experience of ministry in
the church. Almost 500 people in 47 groups joined in
the discussion, and their reflection on the present
priesthood and on women in ministry provided data
for the Second Conference on the Ordination of
Roman Catholic Women.

The decision to organize a second conference was
made in response to the 1977 Vatican *Declaration on
the Question of Admission of Women to Ministerial
Priesthood.* The conference gathered 2,000 women
and men in Baltimore in November of 1978, providing a public forum to protest the *Declaration's* blatant discrimination, to refine and to further
theological reflection on the question of women's
ordination, and to develop strategies for effective
action. In 1982, the Core Commission of WOC decided that a series of local and regional conferences
would constitute the Third International Women's
Ordination Conference whose theme is the Bonding

of Women. These will take place from coast to coast throughout 1982-83.

WOC's bi-monthly newspaper *New Women/New Church* keeps women informed on the state of the question, its own activities and those of local groups, and opportunities for networking. Its contributors inspire and prod to action, as they encourage the readership to study, dialogue and organize in the interests of the ordination of women and a renewed priestly ministry.

Since 1975, WOC has provided a framework for biblical, historical, and theological reflection on one of the church's urgent issues. It has enheartened thousands of women who would leave the church were there no hope that it may someday become a community of equals. A few steps toward the realization of that hope were taken in the dialogue between WOC members and six representatives from the National Conference of Catholic Bishops. Both sides admit to moments of painful impasse in the two-year dialogue, but both sides acknowledge that it was a positive endeavor. The NCCB representatives concluded that:

> WOC represents a Christian feminist perspective calling for the inclusion of women in all ministerial and authoritative roles in the Church. The way that they identified, clarified, and explained major aspects of the issue of women in the Church enlightened and often persuaded us.[15]

They grant, but do not affirm, the traditional

teaching excluding women from priestly ordination and cautiously suggest that perhaps the diaconate might be opened to women. One of the most significant conclusions reads:

> There is need to review the Vatican Declaration on the ordination of women in the light of the insights of modern anthropology, sacramental theology, and the practice and experience of women ministering in our American culture.[16]

The bishops themselves requested an extension of the time limit placed on the dialogue and characterized it as a good model of interaction dealing with an urgent pastoral concern. We sense in these conclusions more than bemused and passive listening, more than mere lip service. There is movement here toward constructive efforts at change. WOC's efforts are largely responsible for this official recognition by representatives of the NCCB of the validity of a Christian feminist perspective.

WOC plays an important role and performs a needed service among Roman Catholic women's groups. It provides one more forum where analysis and action meet and reinforce one another as the church moves slowly toward the realization of its own ideals.

The Leadership Conference of Women Religious

The Leadership Conference lists as its major concerns: the nature of religious life, its place in the church's mission, social justice, the liberation of women, leadership, and collaboration. Its membership of 675 consists of the chief administrative officers of women's religious congregations in the United States. Ninety-one percent of active communities are represented in the organization. Founded in 1956 as the Conference of Major Superiors of Women, it underwent a thorough self-study in 1970-72 from which it emerged with new bylaws and a new name.

The Conference is divided into fifteen regions, and a survey of the concerns and activities of the regions as listed in a recent report indicates a strong commitment to women's issues. Members refer to goals such as the empowerment of women, the removal of sexist language from liturgies, just compensation for women religious, networking, consciousness-raising, and leadership development among minority women.

LCWR has in many ways given voice and visibility to American Catholic women whose experience precisely as women has been largely ignored. Its national study on women and ministry is a notable example.[17] The Conference organized surveys of both women in ministry and of women and men as recipients of ministry. The goal of the project was to document women's experience of themselves in ministerial roles, to determine how women react to the church's ministry to them, and to overcome the unequal status of women in the church. Realizing that the data gathered through the surveys needed interpretation before the Conference could make meaningful recommendations for change, LCWR organized a symposium entitled "Women and Ministry: Designing the Church of the Future." Held in Dayton, Ohio in February 1981, the symposium brought together LCWR members and other church leaders to probe the study's findings and to formulate recommendations for action. The publication that grew out of the symposium[18] includes a summary of findings, commentaries on the methodology employed, responses to the study by theologians, sociologists, and a canon lawyer, and twelve recommendations based on the study's findings and the dialogue that took place at the symposium.

It is an invaluable tool for all who seek a deeper understanding of women's ministry and of ministry to women. It documents the overwhelming predominance of laywomen in ministry, their concentration in traditional "female" activities, and the voluntary character of most of the work they perform. It suggests the under-utilization of women (over 70 percent have never been involved in ministry), and the inadequate preparation (except for those engaged in teaching) of those who do participate in educational, pastoral, and liturgical activities. In one of the most provocative commentaries, Elizabeth Schüssler-Fiorenza concludes that the study's greatest service is to document the extent of the cooptation of women's energies and talents by the patriarchal hierarchy model of church. "The study," she writes, "documents sexism as a structural ecclesial sin on all three levels of church: the economic-social, the theological, and the personal level."[19]

The study, the symposium, and the recommendations that grew out of them are indicative of the role LCWR plays in relation to women's issues. While its membership represents a wide spectrum of opinion in regard to feminist beliefs or strategies, there is agreement on the necessity to sketch as truthfully as possible women's position in church and society and to work toward the greater realization of women's potential in both. At this moment in history it is calling for the admission of women to new ministries, including preaching, the equitable uses of the church's financial resources to support ministry education for women, continued dialogue between and among lay women and women religious, and further canonical and theological study of issues relative to women. The Conference continues to discover what the empowerment of women will entail for women of all economic levels and in all ethnic groups, and it takes concrete steps toward the changes that will help effect it.

NARW, NCAN, WOC, and LCWR are not the only groups which press for justice for women. Women of the Church Coalition brings together eighteen national and local organizations including besides the four mentioned above, the National Black Sisters Conference, Las Hermanas, Institute of Women Today, Quixote Center, the Catholic Committee on Urban Ministry, Center of Concern, Chicago

Catholic Women, 8th Day Center for Justice, Knights of Peter Claver (Ladies' Auxiliary), The Religious Formation Conference, Scapegoat, Tabor House, and Women for Dialogue.

We can safely conclude that feminism is alive and well in the church. Those who get discouraged because progress is slow might take heart from a letter published in *New Women/New Church* in August, 1982. Those who hope that feminism is a harmless fad should be warned. Louella Farmer writes,

> The pain I have felt for years because of the sin of sexism in the Catholic Church was only heightened by the reading of the article on the dialogue between WOC and the Bishops.
>
> I am 65 years old and instead of "mellowing" and accepting things as they are I grow more determined every day that I will fight and work and pray to my dying day to right this terrible sin in my Church which validates it in every other segment of society.
>
> I enclose a contribution which is a huge one for me, a widow with very little income.
>
> Where can I get some blue armbands?

National Assembly of Religious Women
  1307 So. Wabash
  Chicago, IL 60605
  (312)663.1980

National Coalition of American Nuns
   1307 So. Wabash
   Chicago, IL 60605
   (312)341.9159

Leadership Conference of Women Religious
   National Secretariat
   8801 Cameron St.
   Silver Springs, MD 20910
   (312)588.4955

Women's Ordination Conference
   48 St. Marks Pl.
   New York, N.Y. 10003
   (212)777.0890

Chapter Six

WOMEN AND THE FUTURE
OF THE CHURCH

I suggested in the Introduction that any attempt to neatly categorize either today's Catholic woman or today's Catholic church would be foolhardy. Both are in transition. An attempt to characterize the Catholic woman or Catholic Church of tomorrow is equally foolhardy, because the fact that both are in transition does not mean that either will settle into a predictable pattern in the future. And that is a comfort. It attests to the fact that we as church are increasingly prepared to acknowledge and celebrate differences. We may struggle with the limits of pluralism and wonder when it shades off into chaotic *laissez-faire*, but we are not likely either today or tomorrow to return to a prescriptive and deadening uniformity. The methods of the social sciences have made us aware, too, of the critical importance of ethnic, demographic, and socioeconomic factors in any attempt to understand groups in society. And so the same questions I posed at the beginning return at the end: which women? and which church? The church from above or the church from below (to use Hans Küng's categories)? Minority women? White women? Married women? Single women? Lay women? Women religious? Farm women? Urban women? Inner-city women? Suburban women? Old women? Young women?

Is it hopeless, then, to launch into a chapter entitled simply "Women and the Future of the Church?"
Since women do not constitute a group with a single
shared experience, is it futile to focus on women as
such? The question has the merit of recognizing
women's individuality. Nevertheless, the numerous
scholars now concentrating on women's work,
women's writing, women's history, and women's
spirituality recognize that the fact of being a woman
means having a particular kind of social experience.
To be woman has meant historically to belong to a
group for which there are special legal restrictions
and narrowly circumscribed roles. In virtually all
cultures and classes women still lead lives
significantly different from those of their fathers,
husbands, and brothers in terms of access to education, work, leisure, independence, money, power,
and prestige. On the other hand, to be woman has
meant membership in a system whose values differ
significantly, and in rewarding ways, from those of
the prevailing culture. It has meant having the opportunity to develop human attributes and skills admittedly needed, but often lacking, in the public sphere.
In this sense, and without forgetting differences
across class and race lines, it is legitimate to
speculate on women and the future of the church.

My personal hopes for the future of women in the
church are rooted in feminist soil. They are kept
alive by signs that the church of clerics, ranks, and
male hierarchies might be giving way to a church in
which communities of believers share responsibility
and minister to one another according to their gifts.

It is only in this sort of church that women's potential will be realized.

Let us bypass for the moment the enormous task that lies ahead before the transition is complete, both on the level of theory: ecclesiology, nature of community, nature of priesthood, role and personhood, lay ministry; and on the level of pastoral practice: strategies, organization, skills development. Let us instead give free rein to our imagination for a moment.

Growing Up Female in the Church of the Future

At the birth of a female child to Diane and Tom, there is general rejoicing because a "woman" has been born into the world. Her parents' friend, Maria, an ordained member of the parish community, presides at her baptism. The child is called Teresa, after Teresa Avila, Doctor of the Church, whom her parents admire for her intellect, courage, compassion, contemplative depth, and gift for friendship. As Teresa grows up, Tom and Diane consider the relative advantages of the public and private school systems, and decide to send Teresa to the parish school. They like the spirit of community that marks the school and the clear emphasis on the development of values in a religious context. They are also impressed with the teachers' ability to maintain a discipline which does not preclude spontaneity and freedom. They make sure that the curriculum and the textbooks are designed in ways that will support Teresa's growing sense of herself and that will give her as well as her brother, John, every opportunity to develop a strong base in mathematics, science, English, and the social sciences. They encourage her to participate in team sports, one avenue of developing not only good eye-hand coordination but also the human relations skills that will be important in whatever career she chooses later. She begins to deliver papers in the fifth grade and earns enough for the 10-speed bike she wants badly. In sixth grade, Teresa's menstrual cycle begins. She has been prepared for it both by her mother and by the sex education instruction course which started in fifth grade. Diane plans a celebration for her daughter's entrance into a new phase of development. Family and friends rejoice in Teresa's life-giving power, and pray with her that as she moves into sexual maturity she may come to a new awareness and appreciation of herself, and learn progressively what it means to love responsibly and well. They stress that her intellectual, emotional and physical capabilities are all reaching new levels of maturity, and pray that they will grow apace and in harmony.

Teresa considers several high schools and finally, with her parents, decides to attend the local public school because of its variety of programs, dedicated faculty, and excellent facilities. She works on weekends pumping gas at the local station. She and her brother John spell one another off on household tasks such as laundry, dishes, and washing floors.

They both know how to do simple sewing and the
mechanical tasks necessary to keep their bikes and
certain household items in repair. Once a week
Teresa joins her father in a study/action group based
in the parish and reaching out to the community.
The group works at consolidating the gains made by
formerly marginal groups in attaining equality of access to jobs, careers, education, and voice in government, and pushes for further advances. Social
analysis, scripture and theology inform their action.
Teresa develops a taste for both politics and community organization through her work with the
group, and begins to think her life work might lie in
this direction.

As Teresa moves through high school, she struggles with the questions, "Can I love? Am I lovable?
What does it mean to be sexually responsible?" At
home, school, and church she has been encouraged
to view her sexuality not as a dangerous power to be
carefully controlled, but as a means of self-
realization and self-giving. She has accepted as
guidelines the principles that sex should be neither
casual nor exploitative and that its meaning is derived from love. She ponders what love might mean
as she observes the life of others, meditates on scripture, reads widely, and forms close friendships. She
accepts the moral freedom to make decisions in the
realm of sex, and to judge when the nature of a relationship warrants expression in sexual intimacy—a
decision she does not take lightly.

She has a chance to bring up ethical questions not

only about sex, but about social responsibility, medical practice, violence and war in a faith and life-sharing group which meets once a month at different homes in the parish. It joins people of different ages and different economic backgrounds in search of a meaningful faith and in communal prayer. The members take turns leading the discussion and preparing the scripture-based prayer. They support one another in periods of doubt, difficulty, and crisis and celebrate with one another in periods of joy. Two full-time, equally well-paid lay members of the parish staff, Donna and Joe, coordinate this and other similar groups in the parish. They were encouraged by the parish community to a seek a Master's degree from the city's Pastoral Institute, supported by diocesan funds.

Upon graduation, Teresa decides to go to a Jesuit university which provides strong preparation in political science and community organization. Fifteen years before, the university had settled out of court a case brought by women on the faculty charging discrimination on the basis of sex in matters of hiring, promotion, salary, and tenure. In the intervening years, a more equal representation of women has been achieved in most departments. The classroom atmosphere is one where female and male students are given equal attention, voice, encouragement, and respect. Teresa comes to admire and appreciate the professional competence and human warmth of Dr. Janet Pellegrini, head of the Political Science Department.

Janet confirms her in the idea of majoring in political science, and in equipping herself to affect the political process through community organization. Janet is and intends to remain single. She and Teresa speak occasionally about the implications of that choice and of the choice to marry.

The question of marriage becomes real rather than theoretical in her third year at college. By this time, friendship with Marc Schmidt has deepened into love. They decide they will marry, but will wait till he has finished Roman Catholic seminary training and she has begun work in community organization. She will, of course, retain her own name after marriage. She has always taken it for granted that she will work throughout her life, and hopes that her work as a community organizer may have some impact on the life of whatever parish Marc serves.

Let us leave Teresa at this point. She is a woman who has grown to maturity with pride and trust in her own spirit, mind, and body. This serves as a basis for trust in others. Her religious experience has been such that she has a profound sense of the sacred, worships with joy, and makes moral decisions freely and without fear. She will bring a strong sense of identity and life-purpose to her marriage rather than expecting marriage to supply them. She will, hopefully, move through each stage of her life with an increasing self-awareness and growing ability to risk, relate, create, communicte, love and be loved. And with the ability to meet conflict and suffering with courage.

Many elements of this imagined life are possible now. Others represent what women list as important items on the church's agenda in the next five years: recognition of women's right to reclaim authority and accept responsibility for their decisions in the area of sexual ethics, the elimination of sexism in the church and church-related institutions, the ordination of women, a married clergy, and a trained and paid lay ministry. The latter question is one of increasing urgency. It raises questions that will occupy us for the rest of the decade. The answers will affect the lives of both men and women, of course, but here we will explore some of the questions raised from the perspective of women.

Lay Women and Women Religious

For both lay women and women religious the basic question is whether or not their activity constitutes ministry at all. This, however, is becoming an old question. The effort of certain bishops to restrict the term ministry (in its strict sense) to describe the work of the ordained has failed. But the acceptance of women (by definition unordained in the Roman Catholic Church) as ministers raises a host of other questions: How do the ministries of the ordained and unordained relate to one another? What is the status of each? What is the relative status of lay women and women religious? What kinds of ministry are they engaged in? Where? Are they paid? How does their remuneration compare to that of ordained clergy engaged in the same types of work?

The answers, in brief, are that in the church's traditional structures the ordained enjoy a virtual monopoly over jurisdiction, top-level decision making, and sacramental ministry; the ordained are paid more for services than women religious, and women religious are paid more than lay women who often are not paid at all; most women in ministry work in the areas of liturgy, education, and administrative support services, usually in capacities traditionally associated with women; the bulk of parish work is carried on by lay women working part-time as volunteer or low paid workers. These observations are substantiated in the study referred to in the last chapter: *Women and Ministry: A Survey of the Experience of Roman Catholic Women in the United States*, CARA, 1980.

Women in the church, in other words, like women in society in general still occupy low-status and low-paid positions. Women religious, however, generally hold higher positions in the church hierarchy than lay women. This stratification and duality works against the attainment of real equality by any women in the church. It cannot be masked either by lay women who feel that women religious *should* occupy a privileged position (although one subordinate to priests') or by women religious who label it a false issue.

I became conscious of the lay-nun tension at the first Women's Ordination Conference. The main message was that we must pull together, but I felt an undercurrent of resentment at the role that women religious played at the Conference. What was separating us? The feeling, perhaps, that women religious form a semi-clerical caste with social privilege which offsets their minimal salaries? The suspicion that women religious are an obstacle, however unwitting or unwilling, to the attainment of just wages by lay workers and ministers in the church? A lingering suspicion that vowed religious consider themselves superior to married women? Unequal access to higher education as preparation for ministry? An unconscious assumption on the part of women religious that if women were to be ordained, they would be the first and worthiest candidates?

Two of the central issues here are those of work and clericalism. Sisters who gathered at NARW's 10th anniversary meeting devoted much of their time to the first issue. They analyzed women's work in general, and the work of sisters in particular, in a socio-economic and theological framework.[1] They pointed out the disservice to themselves and to all women that results from the tendency of sisters to divorce ideologically their ministry from productive work. By invoking women's special vocation to ministry, pastors can continue to pay subsistence level wages and maintain women religious in positions of economic dependency. Furthermore, a spiritualized definition of labor separates them from the lives of most women workers, dividing a force that would be strong if united. Their willingness to

accept minimal wages (offset by privileged status in
the church) undermines the efforts of lay persons to
organize and push for higher salaries and other
benefits. The conclusions reached at this meeting
and the questions raised are sobering. Women
religious must continue to probe them and to examine their work critically in reference to economic
structures, to power relationships in the church, and
to the work and ministry of all women in traditional
church structures.

Elizabeth Schüssler-Fiorenza has forcefully addressed the issue of clericalism and of the relationship of the lay-nun dualism to different concepts of
church.[2] She sketches two models of church. In one
"lay" (*laicos*) is opposed to "cleric," and refers to the
non-ordained and the non-professional, a subsidiary
and subordinate class. In the second, "lay" is derived
from the Greek work *laos* meaning people. Here,
church is understood as pilgrim people and all of the
baptized are responsible for ministry to one another
and to the world. Distinctions are based not on
gender or on marital status, but on gifts poured out
by the Spirit and recognized by the community. In
the first model, lay women and women religious who
are professionally trained fit neither the description
of lay nor of cleric. Still, women religious, by virtue
of the similarity of their life-style to that of clerics are
"...admitted as quasi-clergy and hold subordinate
paid positions within the parish-diocesan
hierarchy."[3] Meanwhile, lay women move into positions previously held by women religious. This pat-

tern maintains and supports the patriarchal-clerical model of church whereby the unordained are kept in auxiliary ministries while the ordained (exclusively male) reserve sacramental and jurisdictional power to themselves. Women religious, who both ideologically and in practice within their congregations, favor the participatory model thus find themselves in a compromising and contradictory position. Schüssler-Fiorenza sees the women's question, and the lay-nun dualism within it, as central in determining whether the participatory or inclusive model of church will gradually replace the hierarchical model with which it now co-exists. She concludes:

> If the common experience of women in ministry is their economic exploitation and auxiliary subordinate status within the patriarchal hierarchy model of church, then this experience has to become the basis on which the bonding between lay-women and nun-women has to occur.[4]

The response of some women religious and lay women to this realization has been to move out of parish and diocesan-related ministries. They work together in ecumenical groups such as Church Women United or the Institute of Women Today. They staff shelters for battered women, give legal and medical assistance to the poor, join advocacy groups, work with migrants, on campus ministry teams, in hospital ministry and with Peace and Justice Centers. They often seek alternatives to the parish Mass where the language and ritual exclude women or relegate them to the periphery of worship, and where women cannot preach. They have decided to distance themselves from structures in which they feel ignored, misunderstood, used, or wasted and to channel their energy and considerable skills into other works and causes.

Others appreciate the strength and clarity of Schüssler-Fiorenza's argument. They nevertheless find it difficult to reduce their parish or diocesan ministry, admittedly voluntary or ill-paid, to the single dimension of upholding partriarchal structures. They work, study, catechize and pray with parish groups. They gain insight into the religious meaning of their own lives by reflecting on faith and life with others. They press for inclusive language and greater sensitivity to women's issues. They push for collaboration in ministry. They do not accept the unequal position of men and women, lay and clergy, or women religious and lay, but they choose to challenge and change patriarchal structures by their witness within them.

The best trained women, however, seek those parishes and dioceses where there is sufficient scope for their skills in spiritual direction, organization, planning, and group process, and where they share in decision-making. Married women, who are less free to move where these opportunities exist, are at a disadvantage.

Lay women and women religious have common cause in working toward a church in which responsibility and leadership at every level are determined by call, gift, and recognition by the community. We must not, however, assume unity but achieve it by facing squarely attitudes or power relationships which could ultimately keep all of us in subordinate positions forever.

Women and Church As Community

In rejecting positions of subordination determined on the basis of sex women risk being labelled power-hungry. Those whose positions are threatened imagine furious females anxious to do as they have been done to. Those who listen, however, are likely to discover women who may be angry, yes, but who look past anger to ". . . a future not of revenge, which would reproduce the past in reverse, but of freedom, independent action, and the creation of something new."[5] If women are not out simply to replace men in an otherwise unaltered power structure, neither are we content to serve in positions of increasing responsibility with no attendant share in decision-making.

Perhaps the Pastoral Commission of the Sacred Congregation for the Evanglization of Peoples was too quick to conclude that women's requests to be entrusted with greater pastoral responsibilities did not spring from "a spirit of pretension." While women do not want to grab power which robs others of freedom of thought and action, neither do we intend to wait patiently to be told what we will be allowed to do, and where, and under what circumstances. Rather we want to share power as we help invent new ways of exercising it and of empowering others. We want to create new kinds of relationships, those of partnership, in a church where the line between governing and governed is crossed with relative ease.

We want, in other words, to work with those who envision church as community rather than church as chain-of-command.[6] This is the church of the future, and women's traditional sphere of influence fits us admirably to play a central role in it. The abilities to listen, heal, enable, appreciate differences, live with ambiguity, reveal self, give and ask for emotional support, communicate honestly, and to see what is going on below the surface are important in this kind of church. These community-building skills, formerly associated with private life and with women's role, are increasingly seen as essential in the public sphere. And women, still able and willing to offer these gifts, are also asking to receive them. Reflection on power arrangements at home, church, and in society at large have brought women to seek greater mutuality in many areas, in fact, and this at a moment when the church is calling for leadership styles that foster mutuality and collegiality. Women not only have more to gain in structures that are marked by horizontal rather than vertical relationships, we are also more comfortable operating within them.

Our aptness for exercising leadership in tomorrow's church, does not, unfortunately, assure our attaining it. As James A. Coriden points out:

> Ministry is a tightly protected enclave at the leader-
> ship levels. Women are not and will not be admitted
> into the primary ministerial roles or significant
> leadership functions no matter how well qualified
> they are...until one of two things occurs: women
> are accepted as candidates for ordination or leader-
> ship in ministry and the sacrament of orders are
> effectively disjoined.[7]

If neither of these things occurs, more and more
women will choose to exercise their leadership
abilities outside of parish and diocese and the church
of the future will be the poorer for it.

High on the agenda of today's church must be the
resolution to translate into concrete actions and pro-
posals the church's verbal recognition of women's
equality and the bishops' call for an increased role of
women in ministry. Women will experience the
recognition and the call as empty until the full implications of equality are realized. This will involve
paying women what they're worth, affirming women
as individuals and not only as mothers, educating
both women and men in ways which accustom them
to accept women as leaders, and removing limits
which segregate the sexes in the church and in the
world. It will involve psychological and social
adjustments whose dimensions and difficulties we
are only beginning to suspect. It will involve, even,
the slow development of new symbols, ones which
reflect the growing experience of women as central

to ourselves and as image of God.

Progress toward these goals will move the church forward into the future which is in the making even now. The attainment of them has consequences not just for women but for many who are disillusioned and alienated from present structures. The authentic and complete acceptance of women will be a signal that arbitrary divisions at other levels can give way. It will be an indication that warped ideas of sex and of sex-roles have yielded to ones that will lead to wholeness and a healthier self-understanding for all of humanity. It will give powerful witness that the church is ready to live by its own truth and realize its own promise.

NOTES

Introduction

[1]Cited by Sheila D. Collins, "Chains that Bind: Racism, Classism, Sexism," in *New Woman, New Church, New Priestly Ministry*, (Rochester, N.Y.: Kirk-Wood Press, 1980), p 27.

Chapter Two

[1]See Jerome Murphy O'Connor, O.P., *What is Religious Life? A Criticial Reappraisal* (Wilmington, Delaware: Michael Glazier, 1977), pp. 16-30 for a more detailed description of the characteristics of a community of being (as opposed to an action community), and the role of authority within it.

[2]*Daughters of the Promised Land* (Boston: Little, Brown and Co., 1975), p. 315.

[3]See Penelope Washbourne, *Becoming Woman, The Quest for Wholeness in Female Experience* (New York: Harper and Row, 1977), p. 46. Washbourne, herself a wife and mother, insists that women, like men, must forge a personal meaning structure by taking primary responsibility for their own intellectual growth, financial survival, and sexual behavior. They must recognize their potential for a psychic existence that is separate from that of their husbands and children.

[4]*Statistical Abstract of the U.S. Bureau of the Census*, 1980, p. 403.

[5]David A. Schultz in *The Changing Family, Its Function and Future*, 2nd ed. (Englewood Cliffs, N.J.: Prentice Hall, 1976) offers a valuable survey which takes into

account theories of family, cultural differences, experiments in family organization and function, and the need for alternatives to the family as traditionally conceived.

[6]John Paul II, "Laborem Exercens," *Origins*, September 24, 1981, p. 242.

[7]Ibid, pp. 238-240.

[8]John Paul II, "Apostolic Exhortation on the Family," *Origins*, December 24, 1981, p. 445.

[9]Cf. James J. Kenneally, "Eve, Mary, and the Historians: American Catholicism and Women," in *Women in American Religion*, ed. Janet Wilson James (Philadelphia: University of Pennsylvania Press, 1980), p. 195.

[10]*Women, Money and Power* (New York: William Morrow and Co., 1976), p. 100.

[11]"Apostolic Exhortation on the Family," p. 465.

[12]*Handbook, A Call to Action* (Notre Dame, Ind.: Catholic Committee on Urban Ministry, 1976), p. 31.

[13]*Divorce and Remarriage for Catholics* (New York: Doubleday and Co., 1973), ch. XIII.

[14]Ibid., pp. 190-192.

[15]"Apostolic Exhortation on the Family," p. 465.

Chapter Three

[1]"Apostolic Exhortation on the Family," *Origins*, December 24, 1981, p. 448.

[2]Ibid., pp. 447-448.

[3]Of the eighty-two women who responded to this question, only five agreed with the position on birth control stated in *Humanae Vitae*. Many listed this issue as one of the things they found most discouraging or

painful in their church membership. A forty-seven year old mother of four wrote, for instance, "The church's stand on birth control caused us untold anguish in the first eleven years of marriage."

[4]See *Handbook, A Call to Action* (Notre Dame, Ind.: Catholic Committee on Urban Ministry, 1976), p. 66.

[5]Mary Daly places the question of abortion in its social context and in the context of an ethics of sexual caste in *Beyond God the Father* (Boston: Beacon Press, 1976), pp. 106-114. She writes, "A community that is the expression of authentic spiritual consciousness, that is, a living, healing, prophetic religious community, would not cut off the possibility for women to make free and courageous decisions, either by lobbying to prevent the repeal of anti-abortion laws or by psychological manipulation. It would try to *hear* what women are saying and to support the demands for the repeal of unjust laws." p. 112.

[6]New York: G.P. Putnam's Sons, 1981.

[7]"Single Blessedness?" *Commonweal*, October 26, 1979, pp. 588-591.

[8]"Marital Status: ☐ Single ☐ Married," *Daughters of Sarah*, January, 1976, pp. 1-3.

[9]"Apostolic Exhortation on the Family," p. 443.

[10]New York: The Seabury Press, 1974.

[11]*The Church and the Homosexual* (Kansas City: Sheed Andrews and McMeel, Inc., 1976).

[12]Ibid, p. 131.

[13]*Another Kind of Love, Homosexuality and Spirituality* (Chicago: The Thomas More Press, 1977), pp. 146-147.

[14]*Beyond God the Father* (Boston: Beacon Press, 1973), pp. 124-127.

[15]*Gyn/Ecology, The Metaethics of Radical Feminism*

(Boston: Beacon Press, 1978). See especially "The Third Passage," chs. 8, 9, 10.

[16]See "Sexuality and the Church's Liberation," *National Catholic Reporter*, 16 April 1982.

[17]New York: Pocket Books, 1981, p. 36.

Chapter Four

[1]Edward Schillebeeckx, *Ministry, Leadership in the Community of Christ* (New York: Crossroad, 1981). The first three periods are New Testament and patristic times, or the first millenium, the feudal era beginning about the 12th century, and the Tridentine period which spans the 16th century to the present.

[2]Joan Chittister, O.S.B., "Ministry and Secularism," *New Catholic World*, March/April 1980, p. 74.

[3]See Mary E. Hunt, "Roman Catholic Ministry, Patriarchal Past, Feminist Future," in *New Woman, New Church, New Priestly Ministry* (Rochester, N.Y.: Kirk-Wood Press, 1980), p. 31.

[4]Edited by Edward C. Herr (Chicago: The Thomas More Press, 1982).

[5]"Dialog with Church Leaders and Theological Schools on Charisms and Priestly Ministry," in *Women and Priesthood: Future Directions*, ed. Carroll Stuhlmueller, C.P. (Collegeville, Minn.: The Liturgical Press, 1978), p. 162.

[6]*Ministry*, p. 24.

[7]Ibid.

[8]Ibid., pp. 75-104.

[9]Translation from the French in *Crux*, October 4, 1976.

[10]*Powers of the Weak* (New York: Alfred A. Knopf, 1980), p. 15.

[11]*Women's Reality, An Emerging Female System in the*

White Male Society (Minneapolis: Winston Press, 1981). See especially ch. 5.

[12]Ibid., pp. 104-107.

[13]"Ministry in Tomorrow's Church: A Call to Collaboration." Unpublished paper.

[14]"Vocation and Church Ministry: An Overview," *Origins*, November 2, 1978 p. 315.

Chapter Five

[1]*The Subjection of Women* (New York: Source Book Press, 1970. Original copyright 1869), ch. 1.

[2]"Laugh of the Medusa," translated by Keith Cohen and Paula Cohen, 1 *Signs* (Summer 1976): 876.

[3]*Silences* (New York: Delacorte Press, 1978), pp. 27-28.

[4]*Powers of the Weak*, p. 305.

[5]"Spiritual Quest and Women's Experience," in *Womanspirit Rising*, ed. Carol P. Christ and Judith Plaskow (San Francisco: Harper and Row, 1979), p. 231.

[6]Garden City, New York: Doubleday, 1982.

[7]"Why Women Need the Goddess: Phenomenological, Psychological, and Political Reflections," in *The Politics of Women's Spirituality*, p. 73.

[8]"Is a Christian Feminist Theology Possible?" 43 *Theological Studies* (June 1982): p. 282.

[9]36 *Theological Studies* (December 1975): pp. 627-646.

[10]Ibid., p. 639.

[11]Ibid., pp. 642-643.

[12]Cf. "Feminist Theology as a Critical Theology of Liberation," 36 *Theological Studies* (December 1975): 620.

[13]This 1981 "Vision Statement" was the first in which the membership described itself as feminist.

[14]See "Your Daughters Shall Prophesy," *Probe*, September/October 1981.

[15]"Report of the last three sessions of the dialogue between Women's Ordination Conference and the Bishops' Committee on Women in Society and in the Church," *New Women/New Church*, July 1982.

[16]Ibid.

[17]*Women and Ministry: A Survey of the Experience of Roman Catholic Women in the United States* (CARA, 1980).

[18]Doris Gottemoeller, RSM and Rita Hofbauer, GNSH, eds., *Women and Ministry: Present Experience and Future Hopes* (Washington, D.C.: LCWR, 1981).

[19]Ibid., p. 39.

Chapter Six

[1]See *Probe*, September-October 1982.

[2]"We Are Still Invisible: Theological Analysis of 'Women and Ministry,' " in *Women and Ministry: Present Experience and Future Hopes*, ed. Doris Gottemoeller, RSM and Rita Hofbauer, GNSH (Washington, D.C.: LCWR, 1981), pp. 29-43.

[3]Ibid., p. 38.

[4]Ibid., p. 41.

[5]Elizabeth Janeway, *Powers of the Weak* (New York: Knopf, 1980), p. 310.

[6]For an excellent treatment of the meaning of church as community and the challenges involved in forming it see Evelyn Eaton Whitehead and James D. Whitehead, *Community of Faith, Models and Strategies for Developing Christian Communities* (New York: Seabury Press, 1982).

[7]"Implications of the Findings [of the LCWR survey on Women and Ministry] for Preparation for Ministry," in *Women and Ministry: Present Experience and Future Hopes*, p. 58.

BIBLIOGRAPHY

Works Cited and Suggested Readings

Beauvoir, Simon de. *The Second Sex.* New York: Random House, 1974.

Callahan, Daniel. *Abortion: Law, Choice, and Morality.* New York: Macmillan, 1970.

Carr, Anne, B.V.M. "Is Christian Feminist Theology Possible?" *Theological Studies* 43 (June 1982): 279-297.

Catoir, John T. *Catholics and Broken Marriage.* Notre Dame, Ind.: Ave Maria Press, 1979.

Chesler, Phyllis and Goodman, Emily Jane. *Women, Money and Power.* New York: William Morrow and Co., 1976.

Chittister, Joan, O.S.B. "Ministry and Secularism." *New Catholic World*, March/April 1980, pp. 74-79.

Christ, Carol P., ed. *Diving Deep and Surfacing: Women Writers on Spiritual Quest.* Boston: Beacon Press, 1980.

_____. "Spiritual Quest and Women's Experience." In *Womanspirit Rising*, pp. 228-245. Edited by Carol P. Christ and Judith Plaskow. San Francisco: Harper and Row, 1979.

_____. "Why Women Need the Goddess: Phenomenological, Psychological, and Political Reflections." In *The Politics of Women's Spirituality*, pp. 71-86. Edited by Charlene Spretnak. Garden City, N.Y.: Anchor Books, 1982.

Christ, Carol P. and Plaskow, Judith, eds. *Womanspirit Rising: A Feminist Reader in Religion.* San Francisco: Harper and Row, 1979.

Cixous, Hélène. "Laugh of the Medusa." Translated by

Keith Cohen and Paula Cohen. Signs 1 (Summer 1976): 875-893.

Coriden, James A. "Implications of the Findings [of the LCWR survey on Women and Ministry] for Preparation for Ministry." In Women and Ministry: Present Experience and Future Hopes, pp. 55-63. Edited by Doris Gottemoeller, RSM and Rita Hofbauer, GMSH. Washington, D.C.: LCWR, 1981.

Coriden, James, ed. Sexism and Church Law. New York: Paulist Press, 1977.

Coyle, Alcuin, O.F.M. "Dialog with Church Leaders and Theological Schools on Charisms and Priestly Ministry." In Women and Priesthood: Future Directions, pp. 159-176. Edited by Carroll Stuhlmueller. Collegeville, Minn.: The Liturgical Press, 1978.

Daly, Mary. The Church and the Second Sex with a New Postchristian Introduction. Rev. ed. New York: Harper and Row, 1975.

_____. Beyond God the Father. Boston: Beacon Press, 1973.

_____. Gyn/Ecology, The Metaethics of Radical Feminism. Boston: Beacon Press, 1978.

Farley, Margaret. "New Patterns of Relationship: Beginnings of a Moral Revolution." Theological Studies 36 (December 1975): 627-646.

Figes, Eva. Patriarchal Attitudes. Greenwich, Conn.: Fawcett, 1970.

Freeman, Jo, ed. Women: A Feminist Perspective. 2nd ed Palo Alto, Calif.: Mayfield Publishing Co., 1979.

Gilligan, Carol. In a Different Voice. Cambridge: Harvard University Press, 1982.

Goergen, Donald, O.P. The Sexual Celibate. New York: The Seabury Press, 1974.

Gottemoeller, Doris, RSM, and Hofbauer, Rita, GNSH, eds. *Women and Ministry: Present Experience and Future Hopes.* Washington, D.C.: LCWR, 1981.

Greeley, Andrew, ed. *The Family in Crisis or in Transition: A Sociological and Theological Perspective.* New York: Seabury Press, 1979.

Hageman, Alice L., ed. *Sexist Religion and Women in the Church.* New York: Association Press, 1974.

Handbook, *A Call to Action.* Notre Dame, Ind.: Catholic Committee on Urban Ministry, 1976.

Hardesty, Nancy. "Marital Status: ☒ Single ☐ Married." *Daughters of Sarah,* January 1976, pp. 1-3.

Herr, Edward C., ed. *Tomorrow's Church, What's Ahead for American Catholics?* Chicago: The Thomas More Press, 1982.

Hunt, Mary E. "Roman Catholic Ministry: Patriarchal Past, Feminist Future." In *New Woman, New Church, New Priestly Ministry,* pp. 31-42. Rochester, N.Y.: Kirk-Wood Press, 1980.

_____. "Sexuality and the Church's Liberation." *National Catholic Reporter,* 16 April 1982.

Janeway, Elizabeth. *Powers of the Weak.* New York: Alfred A. Knopf, 1980.

John Paul II. "Apostolic Exhortation on the Family." *Origins,* December 24, 1981, pp. 437-466.

_____. "Laborem Exercens." *Origins,* September 24, 1981, pp. 225-244.

Kelleher, Stephen J. *Divorce and Remarriage for Catholics? A Proposal for Reform of the Church's Laws on Divorce and Remarriage.* New York: Doubleday and Co., Inc. 1973.

Kenneally, James J. "Eve, Mary, and the Historians: American Catholicism and Women." In *Women in*

American Religion, pp. 191-206. Edited by Janet Wilson James. Philadelphia: University of Pennsylvania Press, 1980.

McGrath, Sr. Albertus Magnus. *What a Modern Catholic Thinks about Women*. Chicago: The Thomas More Press, 1972. Now available under the title *Women and the Church*. New York: Doubleday and Co., Inc., 1976.

McNeill, S. J. *The Church and the Homosexual*. Kansas City: Sheed Andrews and McMeel, Inc., 1976.

Mill, John Stuart. *The Subjection of Women*. New York: Source Book Press, 1970. Original copyright 1869.

Murphy, Bishop Francis P. "Vocation and Church Ministry: Five Intelligible 'Words'." *Origins*, November 2, 1978, pp. 313-320.

Murphy-O'Connor, Jerome, O.P. *What is Religious Life? A Critical Reappraisal*. Wilmington, Delaware: Michael Glazier, 1977.

Olsen, Tillie. *Silences*. New York: Delacorte Press, 1978.

Peterson, Nancy. *Our Lives for Ourselves*. New York: G.P. Putnam's Sons, 1981.

Plaskow, Judith. *Sex, Sin and Grace: Women's Experience and the Theologies of Reinbold Niebuhr and Paul Tillich*. Lanham, Md.: University Press of America, 1980.

"Report of the last three sessions of the dialogue between Women's Ordination Conference and the Bishops' Committee on Women in Society and the Church." *New Women/New Church*, July, 1982.

Rossi, Alice, ed. *The Family*. New York: W. W. Norton and Co., 1978.

Ruether, Rosemary. *Mary, The Feminine Face of the Church*. Philadelphia: Westminster Press, 1977.

_____. *New Woman, New Earth*. New York: Seabury Press, 1975.

———. Religion and Sexism. New York: Simon and Schuster, 1974.

Russell, Letty. *Human Liberation in a Feminist Perspective: A Theology*. Philadelphia: Westminster Press, 1976.

Scanzoni, Letha, and Hardesty, Nancy. *All We're Meant to Be. A Biblical Approach to Women's Liberation*. Waco, Texas: Word Books, 1974.

Schaef, Anne Wilson. *Women's Reality, An Emerging Female System in the White Male Society*. Minneapolis: Winston Press, 1981.

Schillebeeckx, Edward. *Ministry, Leadership in the Community of Christ*. New York: Crossroad, 1981.

Schultz, David A. *The Changing Family, Its Function and Future*. 2nd ed. Englewood Cliffs, N.J.: Prentice-Hall, 1976.

Schüssler-Fiorenza, Elizabeth. "Feminist Theology as a Critical Theology of Liberation." *Theological Studies* 36 (December 1975): 605-626.

———. "We Are Still Invisible: Theological Analysis of 'Women and Ministry'." In *Women and Ministry: Present Experience and Future Hopes*, pp. 29-43. Edited by Doris Gottemoeller, RSM and Rita Hofbauer, GNSH. Washington, D.C.: LCWR, 1981.

Sennett, Richard. *Authority*. New York: Vintage Books, 1981.

Sheridan, Kathleen. *Living with Divorce*. Chicago: The Thomas More Press, 1977.

Spretnak, Charlene. *The Politics of Women's Spirituality*. Garden City, N.Y.: Doubleday and Co., 1982.

Stuhlmueller, Carroll, ed. *Women and Priesthood: Future Directions*. Collegeville, Minn.: Liturgical Press, 1978.

Swidler, Leonard, and Swidler, Arlene, eds. *Women Priests: A Catholic Commentary on the Vatican*

Declaration. New York: Paulist Press, 1977.

Tavard, George. *Woman in Christian Tradition.* Notre Dame, Ind.: University of Notre Dame Press, 1973.

Trible, Phyllis. *God and the Rhetoric of Sexuality.* Philadelphia: Fortress Press, 1978.

Tuite, Marjorie, O.P. "Your Daughters Shall Prophesy." *Probe,* September/October 1981.

Van Vuuren, Nancy. *The Subversion of Women as Practised by Churches, Witch-Hunters, and Other Sexists.* Philadelphia: Westminster Press, 1973.

Washbourne, Penelope. *Becoming Woman, The Quest for Wholeness in Female Experience.* New York: Harper and Row, 1977.

Weaver, Mary Jo. "Single Blessedness?" *Commonweal,* October 26, 1979, pp. 588-591.

Whitehead, Evelyn Eaton, ed. *The Parish in Community and Ministry.* New York: Paulist Press, 1978.

Whitehead, Evelyn Eaton and Whitehead, James D. *Community of Faith, Models and Strategies for Developing Christian Communities.* New York: Seabury Press, 1982.

Whitehead, James D. and Whitehead, Evelyn Eaton. *Marrying Well: Possibilities in Christian Marriage Today.* New York: Doubleday and Co., 1981.

Women and Ministry: A Survey of the Experience of Roman Catholic Women in the United States. CARA, 1980.

Wood, Frederic C., Jr. *Sex and the New Morality.* New York: Association Press, 1974.

Woods, Richard. *Another Kind of Love, Homosexuality and Spirituality.* Chicago: The Thomas More Press, 1977.

Young, James J., C.S.P., ed. *Ministering to the Divorced Catholic.* New York: Paulist Press, 1979.